Every word of God is pure:
He is a shield unto them
that put their trust in him.
-Proverbs 30:5

Prayer

God give me the peace of
mind to accept the changes in
my life that I cannot control;
the fortitude and faith
to change what is within
my control; and
the spiritual discernment
to know the difference.

SPIRIT GUIDE MY FEET

DATE

But the Advocate, the Holy Spirit...will teach you all things and will remind you of everything...John 14:26

HOLY SPIRIT THANK YOU FOR:

HOLY SPIRIT teach me...

HOLY SPIRIT remind me...

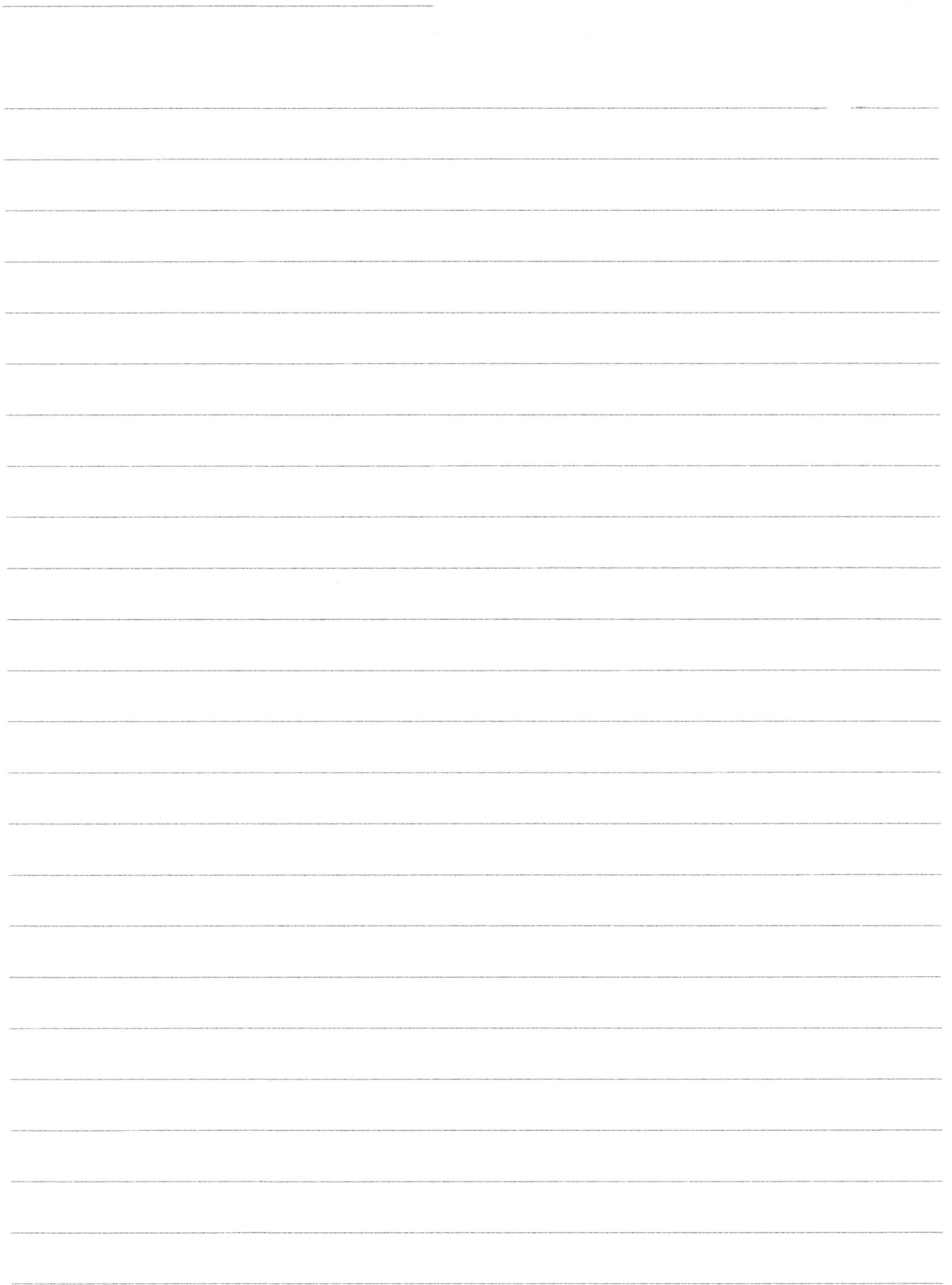

Proverbs 31 Verse 10: Who can find a virtuous woman? For her worth is far above rubies.

In this moment, I am Grateful for

_____
_____
_____
_____
_____
_____

Date

_____

People To Pray For

_____
_____
_____
_____
_____
_____
_____
_____
_____
_____
_____
_____
_____
_____
_____

Personal Challenges

_____
_____
_____
_____
_____

Prayers for Our Government

_____
_____
_____
_____
_____

Reflections

_____
_____
_____
_____
_____

Prayer of Jabez

"Jabez cried out to the God of
Israel, "Oh that You would
bless
me and enlarge my territory!
Let your hand be with me, and
keep me from
harm so that I will be free
from pain." And God granted
his request."

1 Chronicles 4:10

Random Thoughts, ideas, and inspirations...

SPIRIT GUIDE MY FEET

DATE

But the Advocate, the Holy Spirit...will teach you all things and will remind you of everything...John 14:26

HOLY SPIRIT THANK YOU FOR:

HOLY SPIRIT TEACH ME...

HOLY SPIRIT REMIND ME...

Proverbs 31 Verse 12: She does him good and not evil All the days of her life.

_____

_____

_____

_____

_____

_____

_____

_____

_____

_____

_____

_____

_____

_____

_____

_____

_____

_____

_____

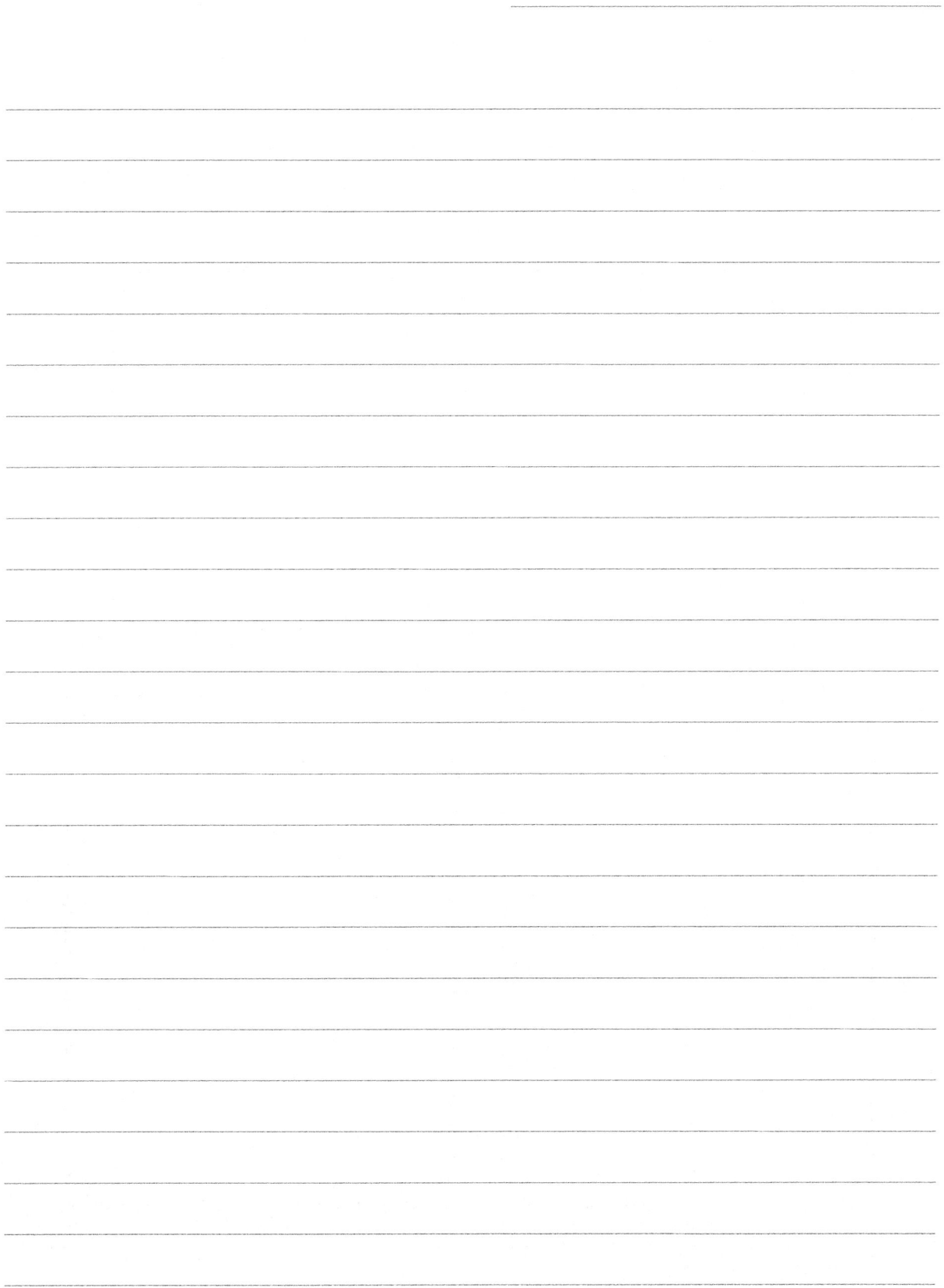

SPIRIT GUIDE MY FEET

DATE

But the Advocate, the Holy Spirit...will teach you all things and will remind you of everything...John 14:26

HOLY SPIRIT THANK YOU FOR:

HOLY SPIRIT teach me...

HOLY SPIRIT remind me...

Proverbs 31 Verse 17: She girds herself with strength, and strengthens her arms. From her profits she plants a vineyard. Her clothing is fine linen and purple.

_____

_____

_____

_____

_____

_____

_____

_____

_____

_____

_____

_____

_____

_____

_____

_____

_____

_____

The Lord's Prayer

After this manner therefore pray ye: Our Father which art in heaven, Hallowed be thy name. Thy kingdom come, Thy will be done in earth, as it is in heaven. Give us this day our daily bread. And forgive us our debts, as we forgive our debtors. And lead us not into temptation, but deliver us from evil: For thine is the kingdom, and the power, and the glory, for ever. Amen.

Matthew 6:9-13

Random Thoughts, ideas, and inspirations...

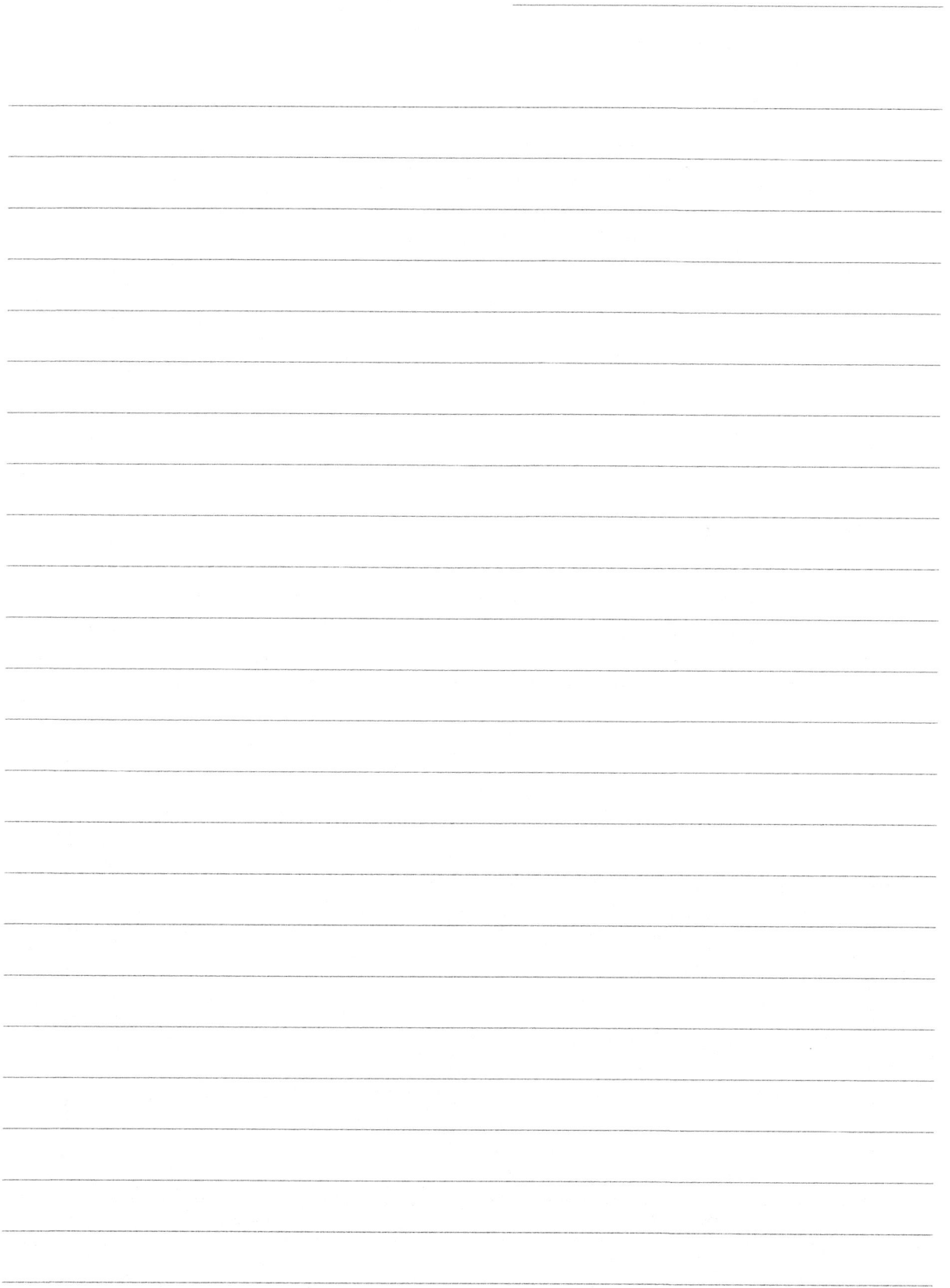

SPIRIT GUIDE MY FEET

DATE

But the Advocate, the Holy Spirit...will teach you all things and will remind you of everything...John 14:26

Holy Spirit Thank You For:

Holy Spirit teach me...

Holy Spirit remind me...

Proverbs 31 Verse 21: She is not afraid of snow for her household, For all her household is clothed with scarlet.

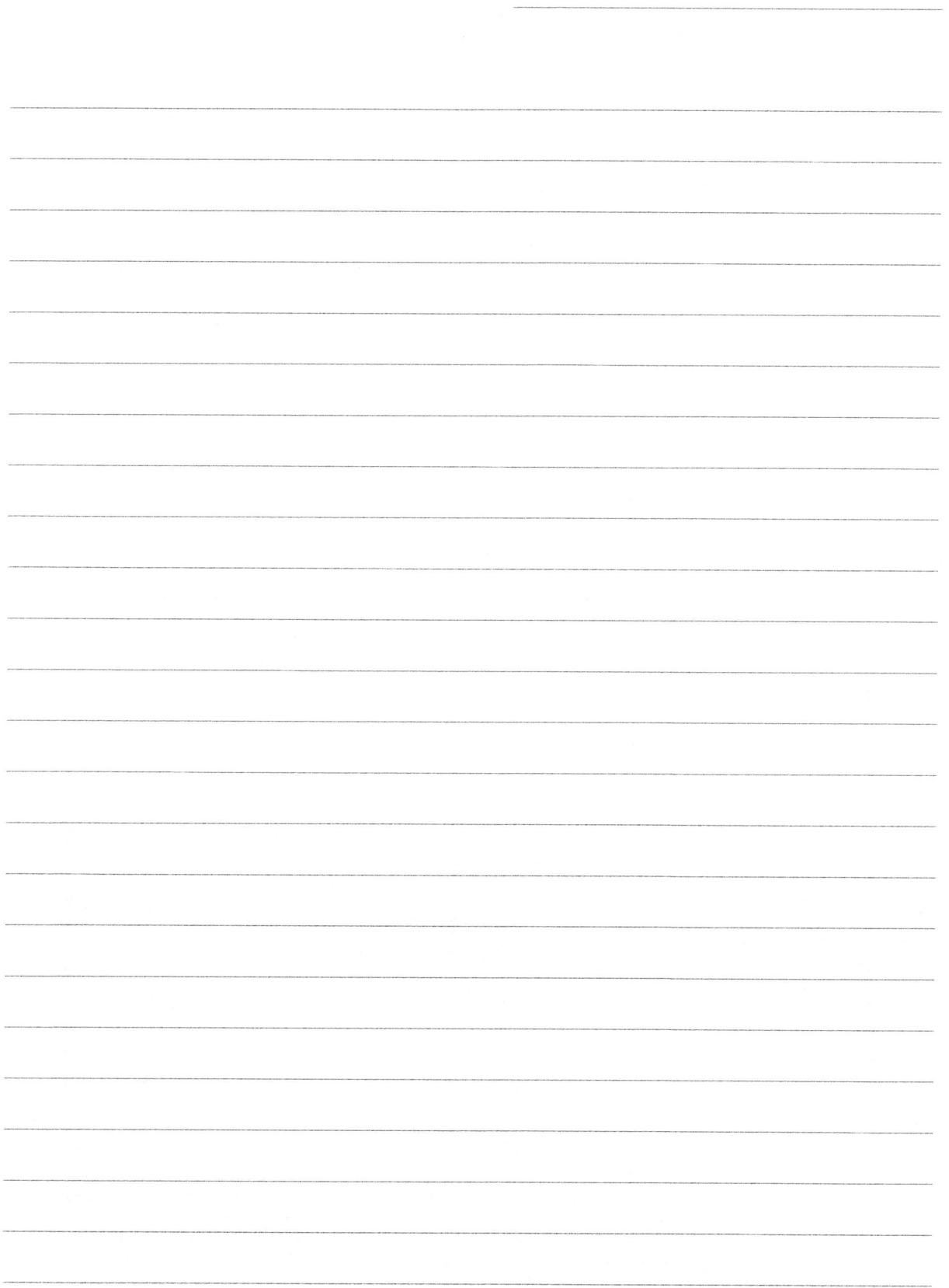

SPIRIT GUIDE MY FEET

DATE

But the Advocate, the Holy Spirit...will teach you all things and will remind you of everything...John 14:26

HOLY SPIRIT THANK YOU FOR:

HOLY SPIRIT TEACH ME...

HOLY SPIRIT REMIND ME...

Proverbs 31 Verse 11: The heart of her husband safely trusts her.

Random Thoughts, ideas, and inspirations...

In this moment, I am Grateful for

_____
_____
_____
_____
_____
_____

Personal Challenges

_____
_____
_____
_____
_____
_____

Prayers for Our Government

_____
_____
_____
_____
_____

Reflections

Date

_____

People To Pray For

_____
_____
_____
_____
_____
_____
_____
_____
_____
_____
_____
_____
_____
_____
_____

_____
_____
_____
_____
_____

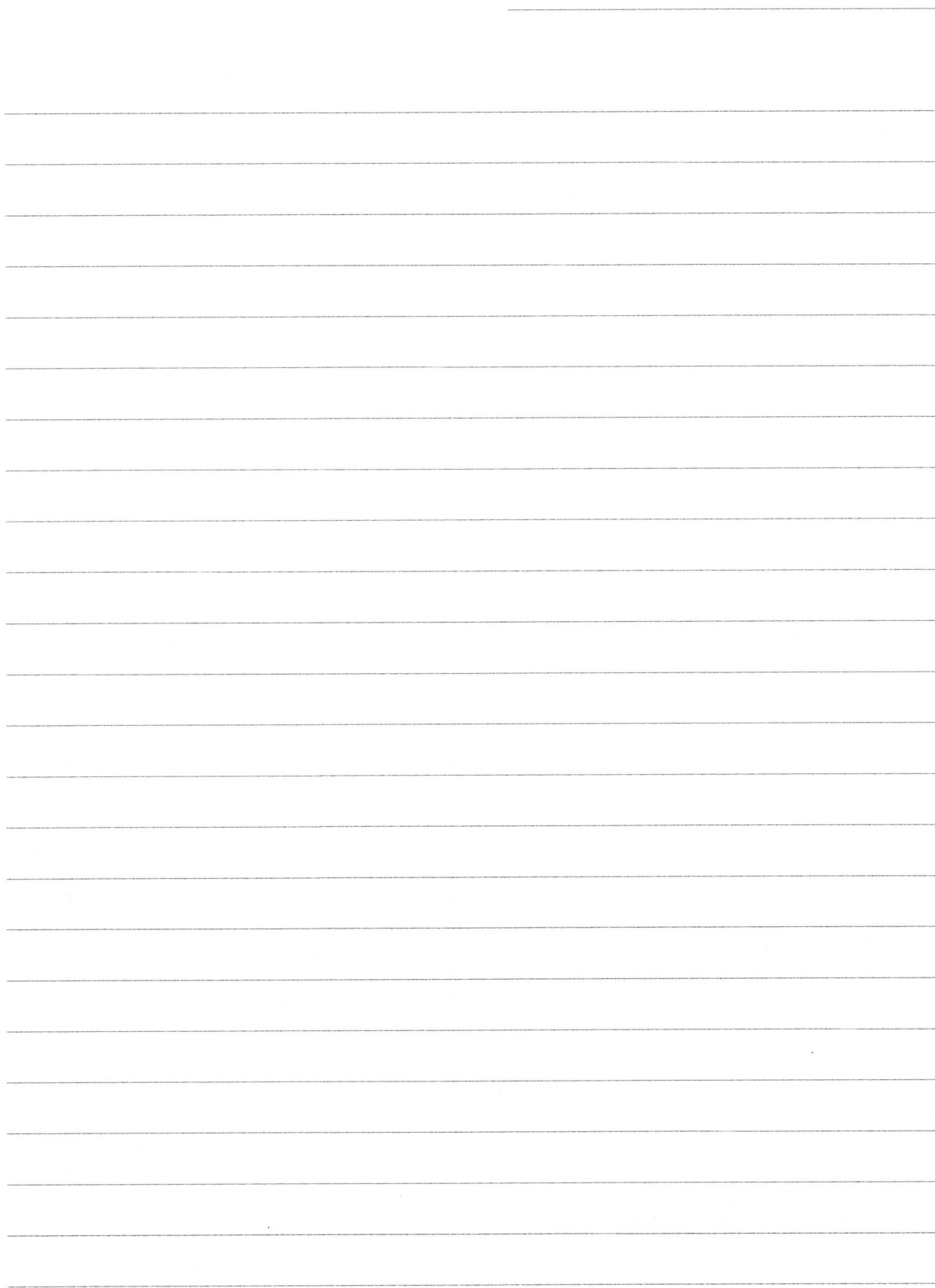

SPIRIT GUIDE MY FEET

DATE

But the Advocate, the Holy Spirit...will teach you all things and will remind you of everything...John 14:26

HOLY SPIRIT THANK YOU FOR:

HOLY SPIRIT teach me...

HOLY SPIRIT remind me...

Proverbs 31 Verse 14: She is like the merchant ships, She brings her food from afar.

Random Thoughts, ideas, and inspirations...

In this moment, I am Grateful for

_____
_____
_____
_____
_____
_____

Date

_____

People To Pray For

_____
_____
_____
_____
_____
_____
_____
_____
_____
_____
_____
_____
_____
_____

Personal Challenges

_____
_____
_____
_____
_____

Prayers for Our Government

_____
_____
_____
_____
_____

Reflections

_____
_____
_____
_____
_____

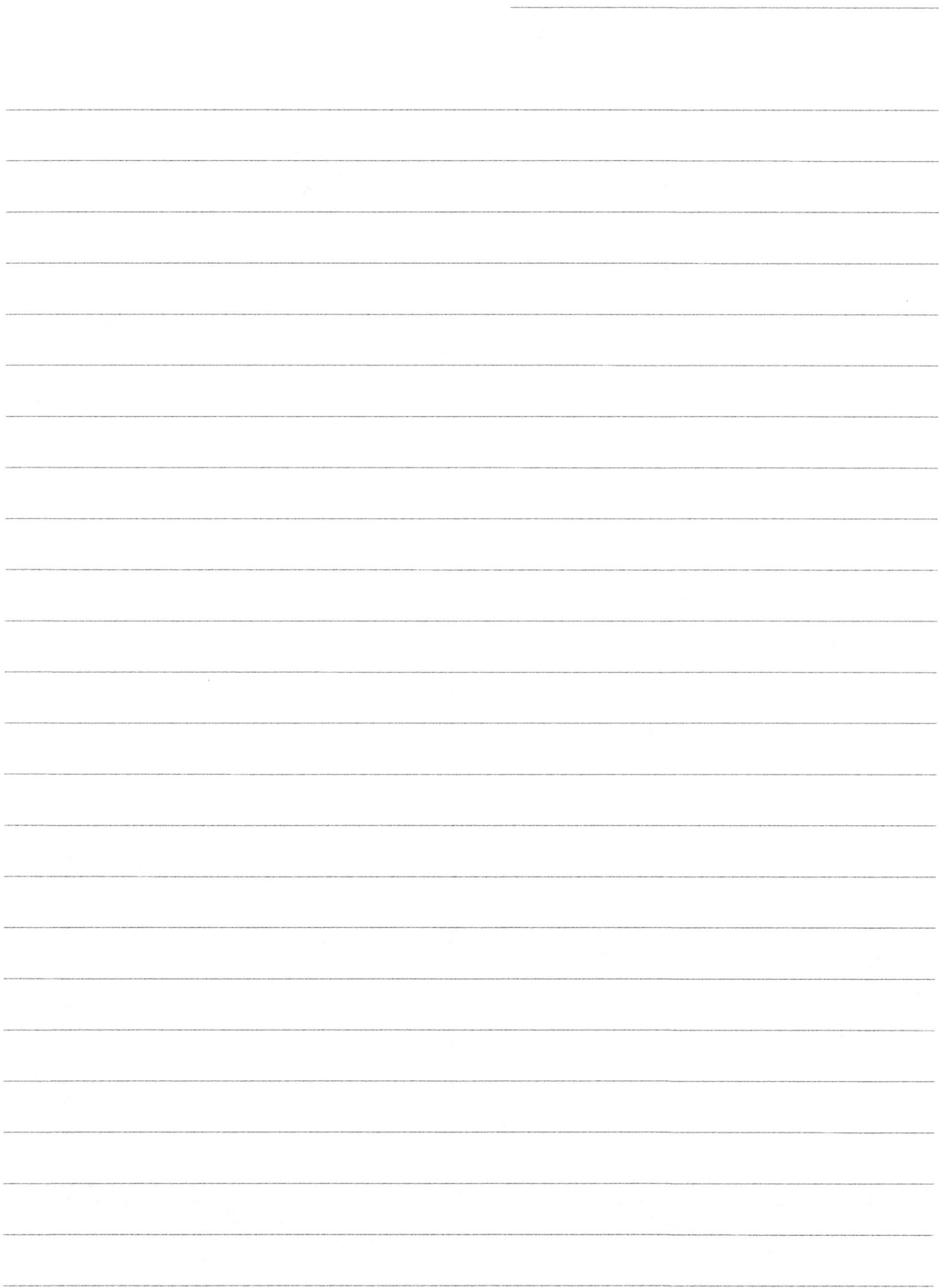

SPIRIT GUIDE MY FEET

DATE

But the Advocate, the Holy Spirit...will teach you all things and will remind you of everything...John 14:26

HOLY SPIRIT THANK YOU FOR:

HOLY SPIRIT TEACH ME...

HOLY SPIRIT REMIND ME...

Proverbs 31 Verse 30: Charm is deceitful and beauty is passing, but a woman who fears the Lord, she shall be praised. So he will have no lack of gain.

Random Thoughts, ideas, and inspirations...

In this moment, I am Grateful for

_____

_____

_____

_____

_____

Date

_____

People To Pray For

_____

_____

_____

_____

_____

Personal Challenges

_____

_____

_____

_____

_____

_____

_____

_____

_____

_____

_____

_____

_____

_____

_____

Prayers for Our Government

_____

_____

_____

_____

_____

Reflections

_____

_____

_____

_____

_____

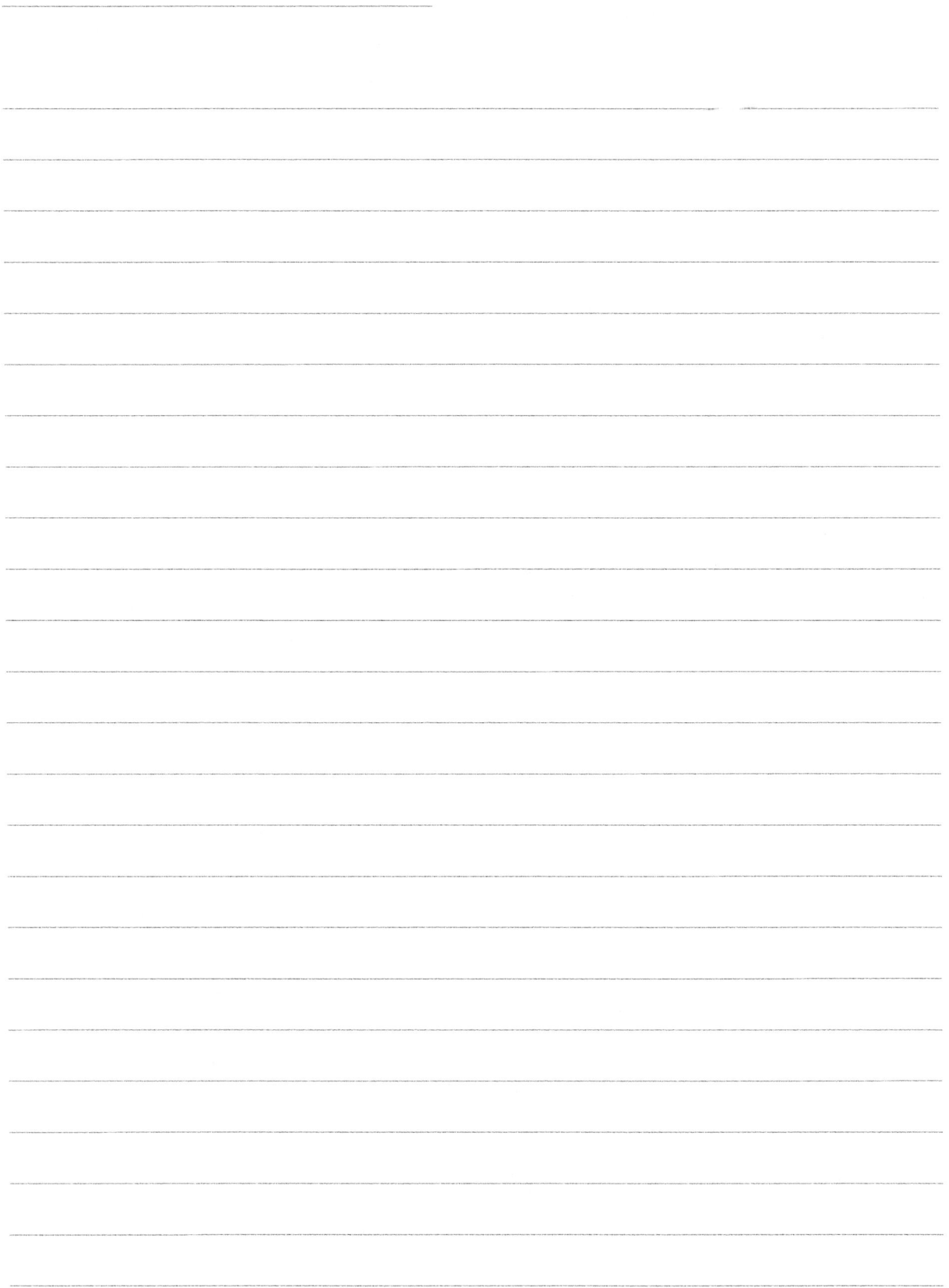

SPIRIT GUIDE MY FEET

DATE

But the Advocate, the Holy Spirit...will teach you all
things and will remind you of everything...John 14:26

HOLY SPIRIT THANK YOU FOR:

HOLY SPIRIT TEACH ME...

HOLY SPIRIT REMIND ME...

Proverbs 31 Verse 23: Her husband is known in the gates, when he sits among the elders of the land.

Random Thoughts, ideas, and inspirations...

In this moment, I am Grateful for

Date

_____

_____

_____

_____

_____

People To Pray For

Personal Challenges

_____

_____

_____

_____

_____

Prayers for Our Government

_____

_____

_____

_____

Reflections

_____

_____

_____

_____

SPIRIT GUIDE MY FEET

DATE

But the Advocate, the Holy Spirit...will teach you all things and will remind you of everything...John 14:26

HOLY SPIRIT THANK YOU FOR:

HOLY SPIRIT teach me...

HOLY SPIRIT remind me...

Proverbs 31 Verse 22: She makes tapestry for herself.

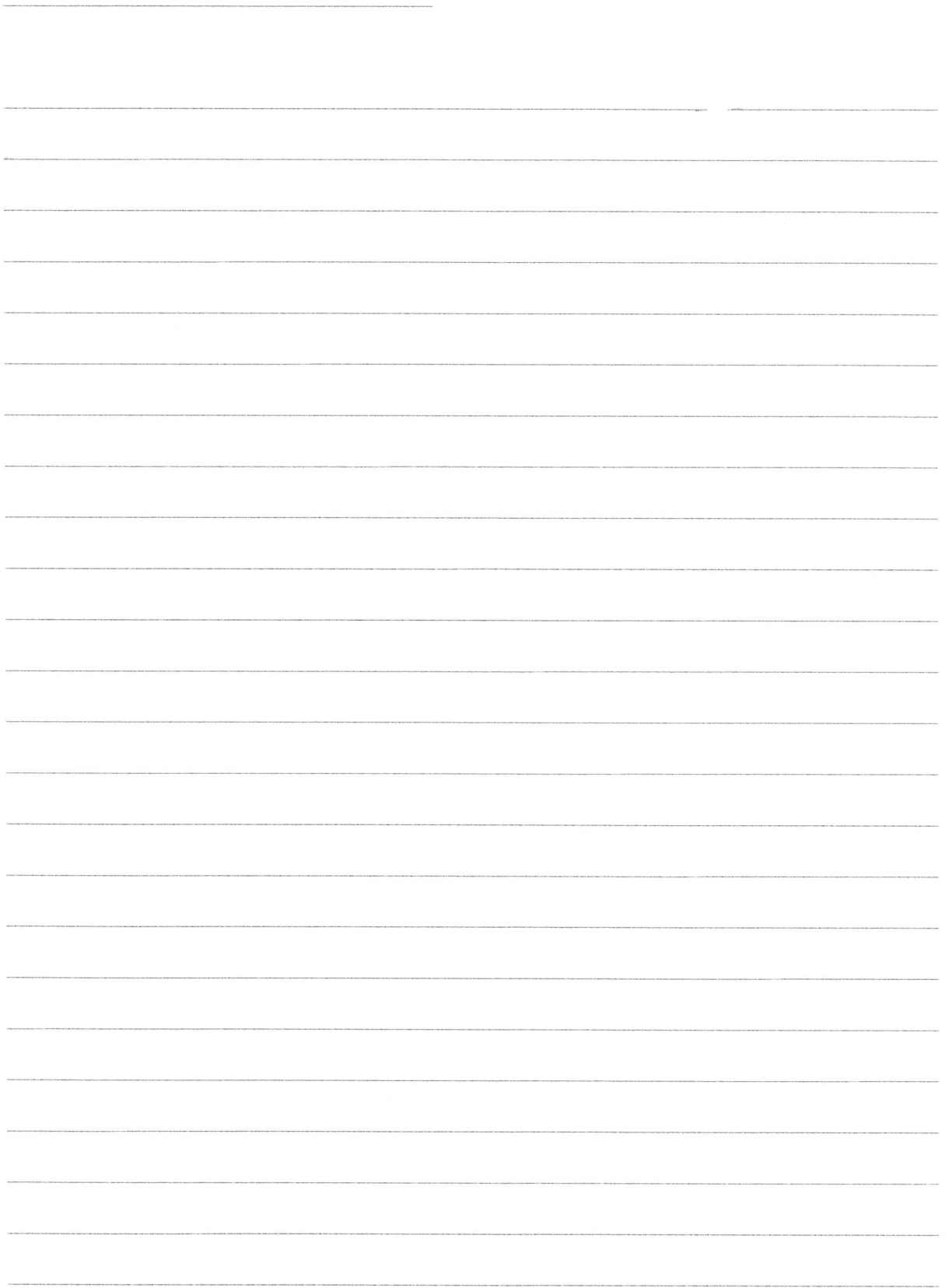

SPIRIT GUIDE MY FEET

DATE

But the Advocate, the Holy Spirit...will teach you all things and will remind you of everything...John 14:26

Holy Spirit Thank You For:

Holy Spirit teach me...

Holy Spirit remind me...

Proverbs 31 Verse 26: She opens her mouth with wisdom, And on her tongue is the law of kindness.

Random Thoughts, ideas, and inspirations...

In this moment, I am Grateful for

_____
_____
_____
_____
_____

Personal Challenges

_____
_____
_____
_____
_____

Prayers for Our Government

_____
_____
_____
_____
_____

Reflections

Date

_____

People To Pray For

_____
_____
_____
_____
_____
_____
_____
_____
_____
_____
_____
_____
_____
_____

_____
_____
_____
_____
_____

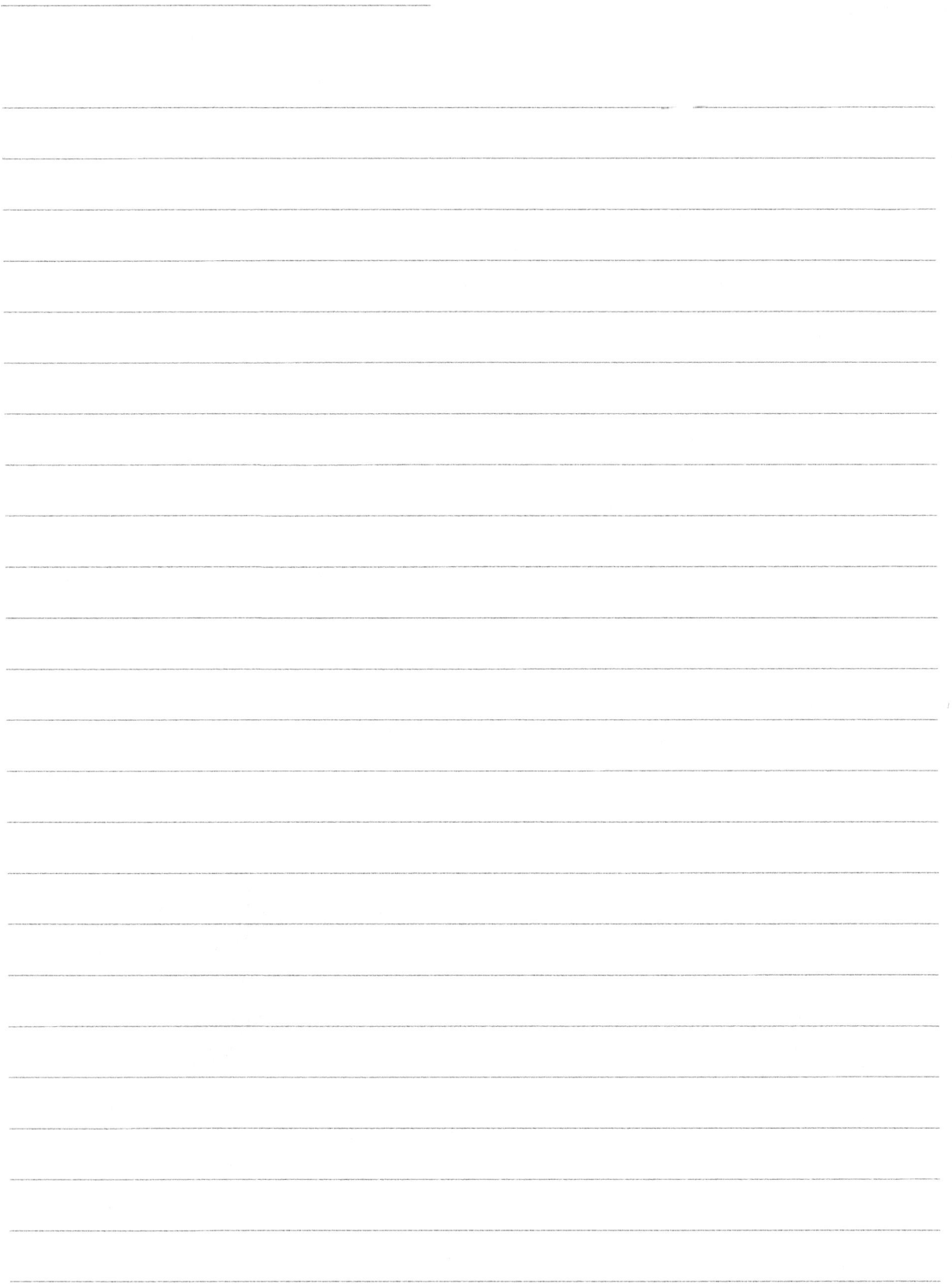

SPIRIT GUIDE MY FEET

DATE

But the Advocate, the Holy Spirit...will teach you all things and will remind you of everything...John 14:26

HOLY SPIRIT THANK YOU FOR:

HOLY SPIRIT TEACH ME...

HOLY SPIRIT REMIND ME...

Proverbs 31 Verse 20: She extends her hand to the poor, Yes, she reaches out her hands to the needy.

SPIRIT GUIDE MY FEET

DATE

But the Advocate, the Holy Spirit...will teach you all things and will remind you of everything...John 14:26

HOLY SPIRIT THANK YOU FOR:

HOLY SPIRIT TEACH ME...

HOLY SPIRIT REMIND ME...

Proverbs 31 Verse 15: She also rises while it is yet night, And provides food for her household, And a portion for her maidservants.

Random Thoughts, ideas, and inspirations...

In this moment, I am Grateful for

_____
_____
_____
_____
_____
_____

Personal Challenges

_____
_____
_____
_____
_____
_____

Prayers for Our Government

_____
_____
_____
_____
_____

Reflections

Date

_____

People To Pray For

_____
_____
_____
_____
_____
_____
_____
_____
_____
_____
_____
_____
_____
_____
_____

_____
_____
_____
_____
_____

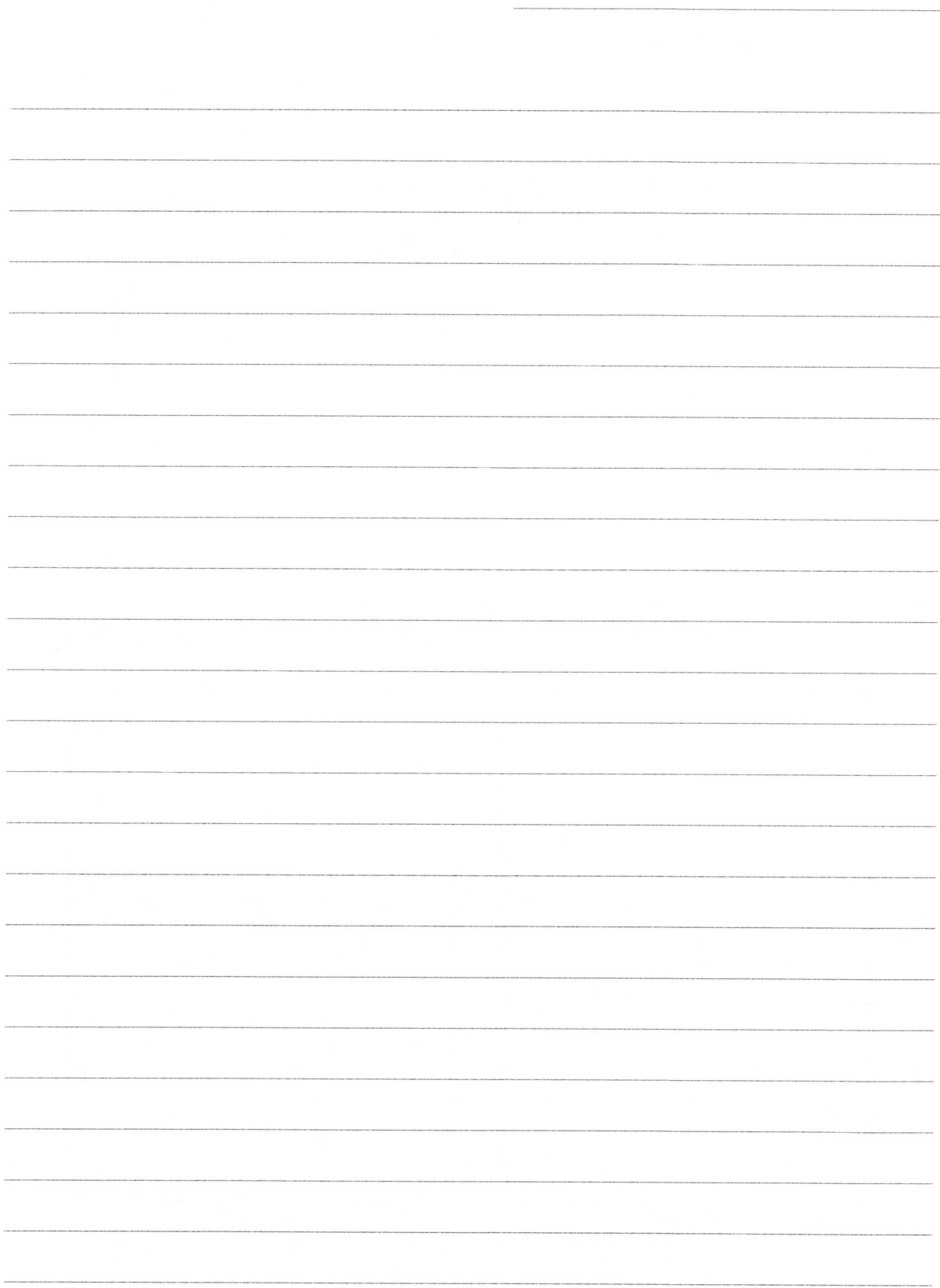

SPIRIT GUIDE MY FEET

DATE

But the Advocate, the Holy Spirit...will teach you all things and will remind you of everything...John 14:26

Holy Spirit Thank You For:

Holy Spirit teach me...

Holy Spirit remind me...

Proverbs 31 Verse 24: She makes linen garments and sells them, And supplies sashes for the merchants.

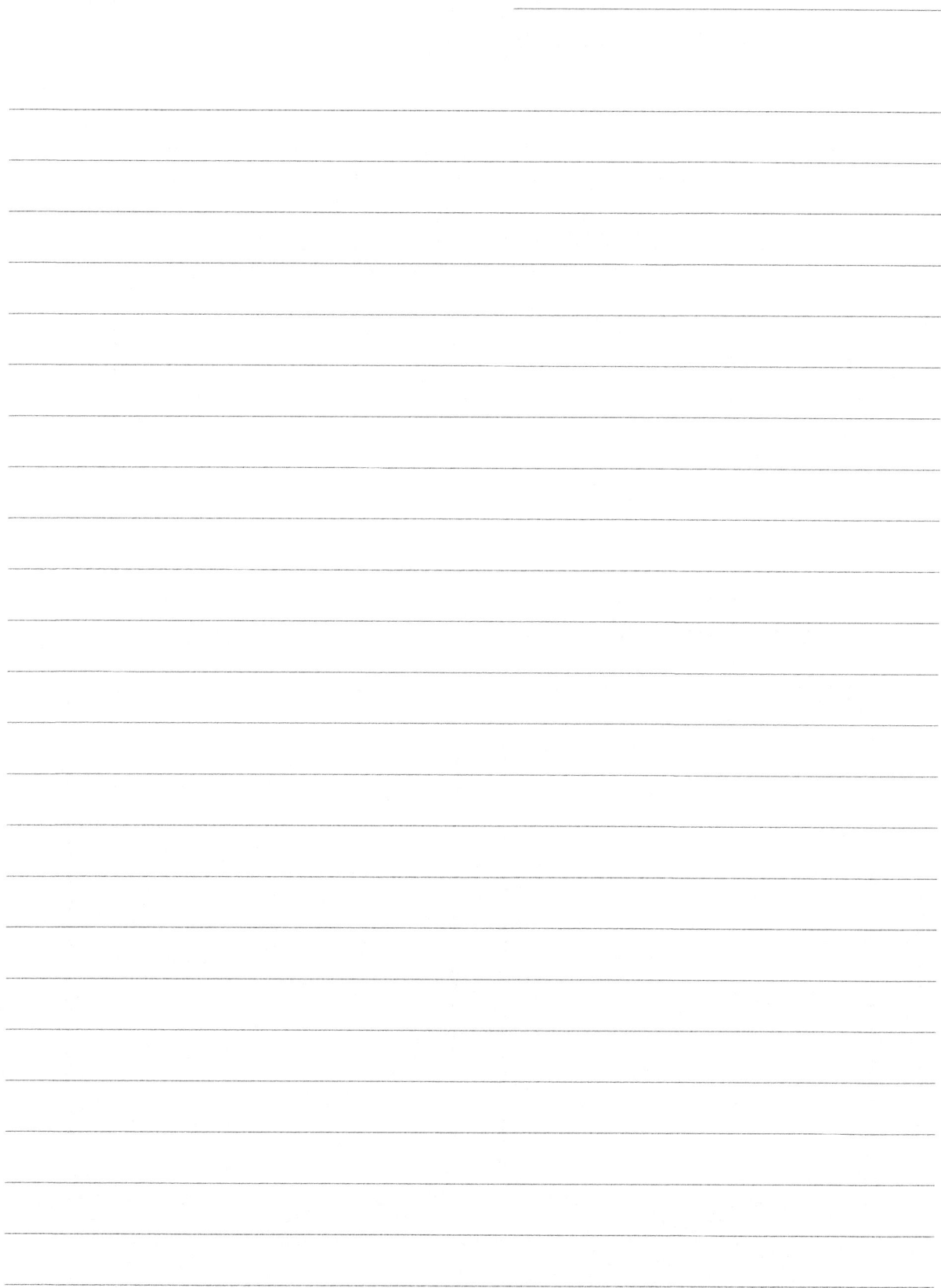

SPIRIT GUIDE MY FEET

DATE

But the Advocate, the Holy Spirit...will teach you all
things and will remind you of everything...John 14:26

Holy Spirit Thank You For:

Holy Spirit teach me...

Holy Spirit remind me...

Proverbs 31 Verse 25: Strength and honor are her clothing.

Random Thoughts, ideas, and inspirations...

In this moment, I am Grateful for

_____
_____
_____
_____
_____
_____

Date

_____

People To Pray For

_____
_____
_____
_____
_____
_____
_____
_____
_____
_____
_____
_____
_____
_____
_____

Personal Challenges

_____
_____
_____
_____
_____
_____

Prayers for Our Government

_____
_____
_____
_____
_____
_____

Reflections

_____
_____
_____
_____
_____

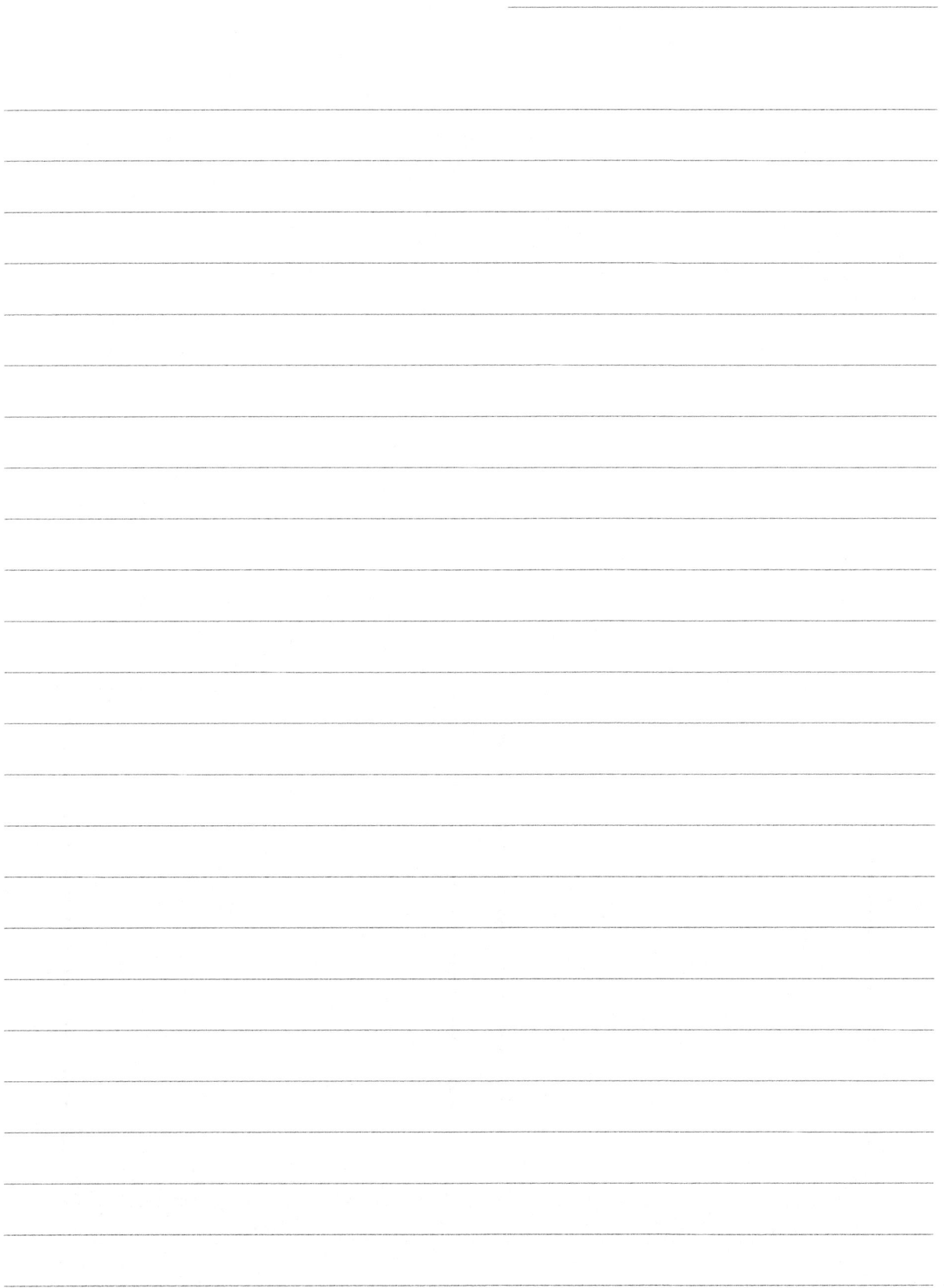

SPIRIT GUIDE MY FEET

DATE

But the Advocate, the Holy Spirit...will teach you all things and will remind you of everything...John 14:26

Holy Spirit Thank You For:

Holy Spirit teach me...

Holy Spirit remind me...

Proverbs 31 Verse 31: Give her of the fruit of her hands, And let her own works praise her in the gates.

SPIRIT GUIDE MY FEET

DATE

But the Advocate, the Holy Spirit...will teach you all things and will remind you of everything...John 14:26

Holy Spirit Thank You For:

Holy Spirit teach me...

Holy Spirit remind me...

Proverbs 31 Verse 29: Many daughters have done well, but you excel them all."Her husband also, and he praises her:

_____

_____

_____

_____

_____

_____

_____

_____

_____

_____

_____

_____

_____

_____

_____

_____

_____

_____

In this moment, I am Grateful for

_____
_____
_____
_____
_____
_____

Date

_____

People To Pray For

_____
_____
_____
_____
_____
_____
_____
_____
_____
_____
_____
_____
_____
_____
_____

Personal Challenges

_____
_____
_____
_____
_____

Prayers for Our Government

_____
_____
_____
_____
_____

Reflections

_____
_____
_____
_____
_____

Random Thoughts, ideas, and inspirations...

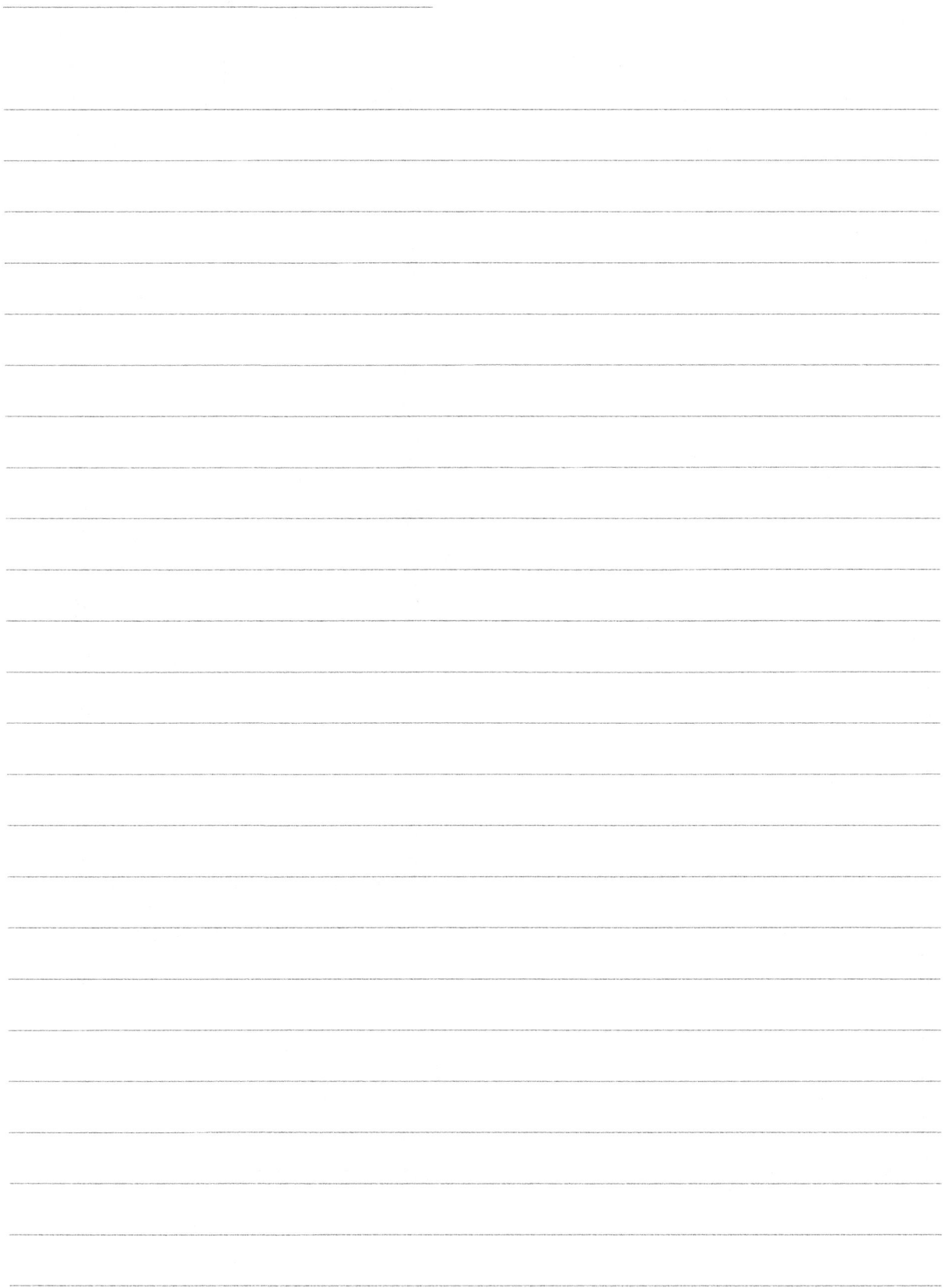

SPIRIT GUIDE MY FEET

DATE

But the Advocate, the Holy Spirit...will teach you all
things and will remind you of everything...John 14:26

Holy Spirit Thank You For:

Holy Spirit teach me...

Holy Spirit remind me...

Proverbs 31 Verse 27: She watches over the ways of her household,
And does not eat the bread of idleness.

SPIRIT GUIDE MY FEET

DATE

But the Advocate, the Holy Spirit...will teach you all things and will remind you of everything...John 14:26

Holy Spirit Thank You For:

Holy Spirit teach me...

Holy Spirit remind me...

Proverbs 31 Verse 19: She stretches out her hands to the distaff, And her hand holds the spindle.

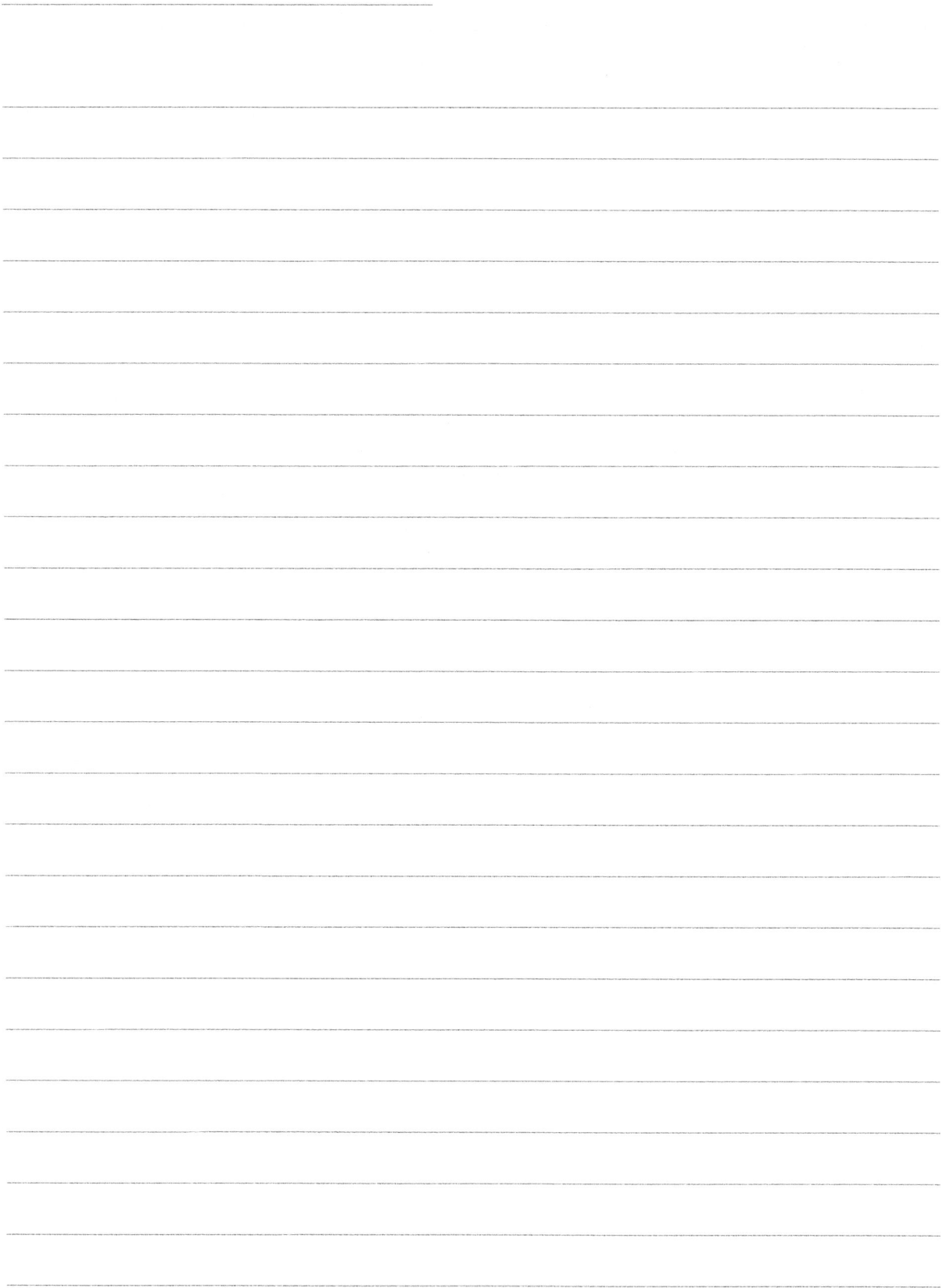

Random Thoughts, ideas, and inspirations...

In this moment, I am Grateful for

_____
_____
_____
_____
_____
_____

Personal Challenges

_____
_____
_____
_____
_____
_____

Prayers for Our Government

_____
_____
_____
_____
_____

Reflections

Date

_____

People To Pray For

_____
_____
_____
_____
_____
_____
_____
_____
_____
_____
_____
_____
_____
_____
_____
_____

_____
_____
_____
_____
_____

SPIRIT GUIDE MY FEET

DATE

But the Advocate, the Holy Spirit...will teach you all
things and will remind you of everything...John 14:26

HOLY SPIRIT THANK YOU FOR:

HOLY SPIRIT teach me...

HOLY SPIRIT remind me...

Proverbs 31 Verse 28: Her children rise up and call her blessed.

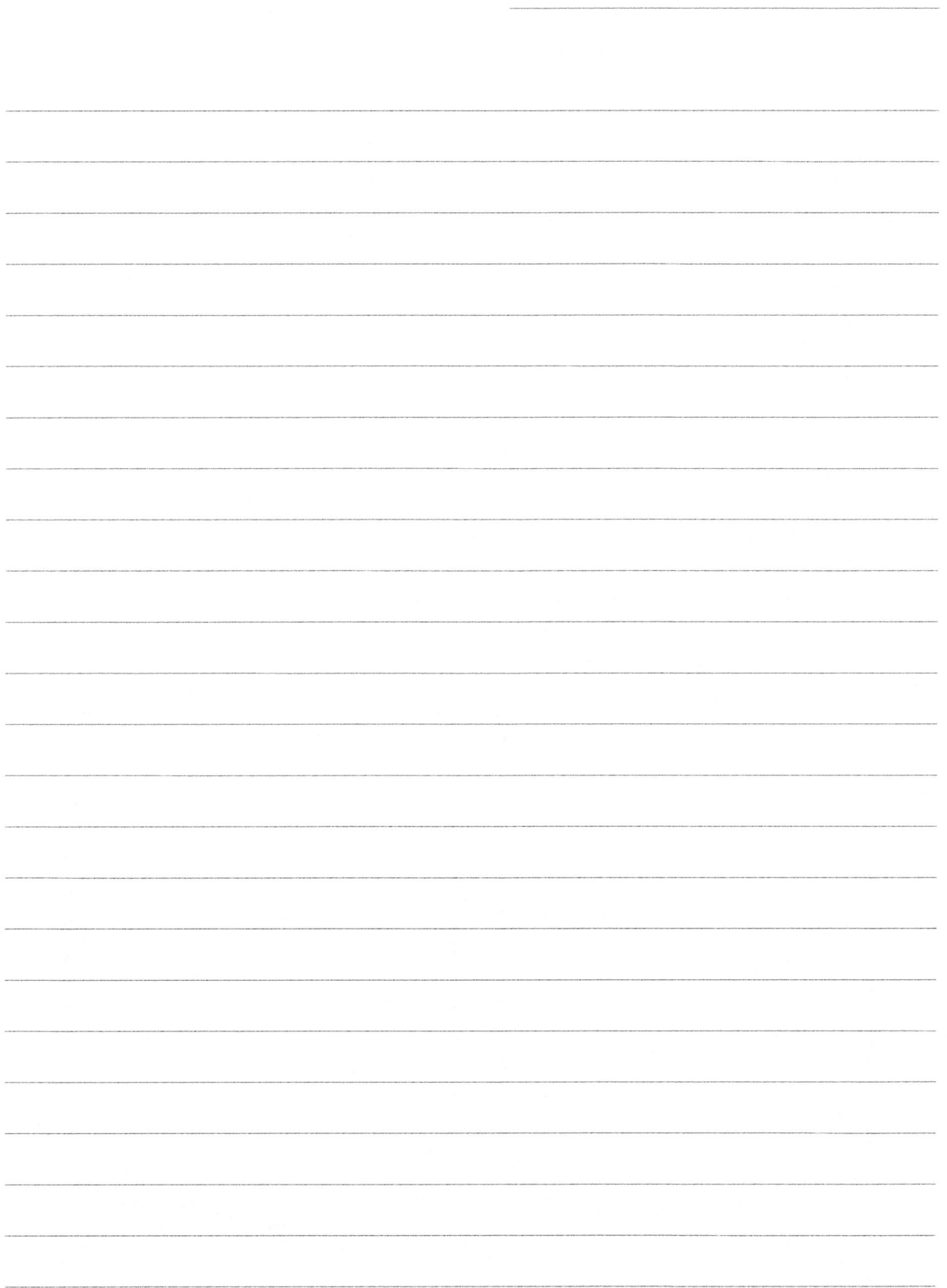

SPIRIT GUIDE MY FEET

DATE

But the Advocate, the Holy Spirit...will teach you all
things and will remind you of everything...John 14:26

HOLY SPIRIT THANK YOU FOR:

HOLY SPIRIT TEACH ME...

HOLY SPIRIT REMIND ME...

Proverbs 31 Verse 13: She seeks wool and flax, and willingly works with her hands. She shall rejoice in time to come.

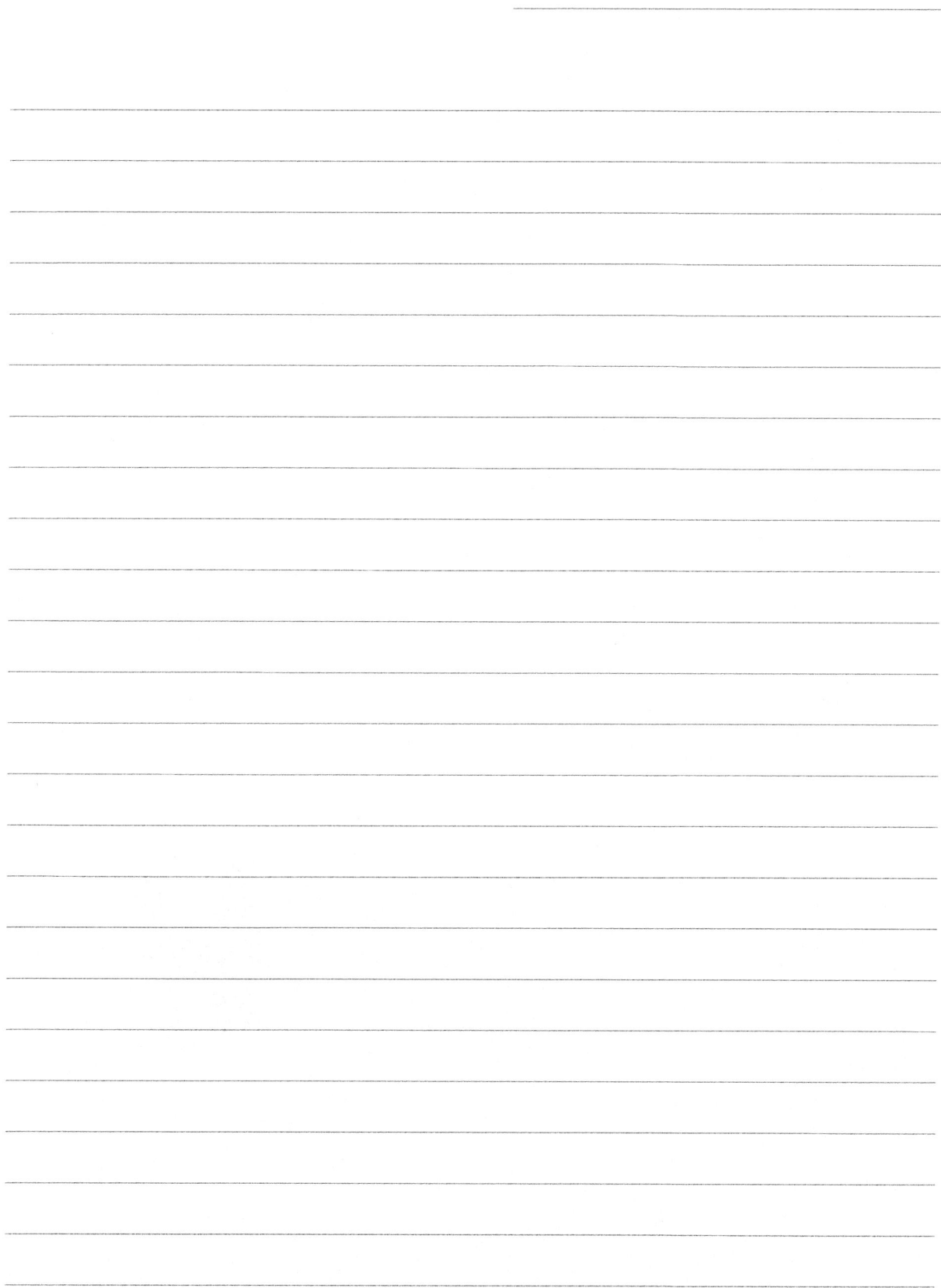

In this moment, I am Grateful for

_____
_____
_____
_____
_____

Personal Challenges

_____
_____
_____
_____
_____

Prayers for Our Government

_____
_____
_____
_____
_____

Reflections

_____
_____
_____
_____
_____

Date

_____

People To Pray For

_____
_____
_____
_____
_____
_____
_____
_____
_____
_____
_____
_____
_____
_____
_____
_____

Random Thoughts, ideas, and inspirations...

SPIRIT GUIDE MY FEET

DATE

But the Advocate, the Holy Spirit...will teach you all things and will remind you of everything...John 14:26

Holy Spirit Thank You For:

Holy Spirit teach me...

Holy Spirit remind me...

Proverbs 31 Verse 16: She considers a field and buys it.

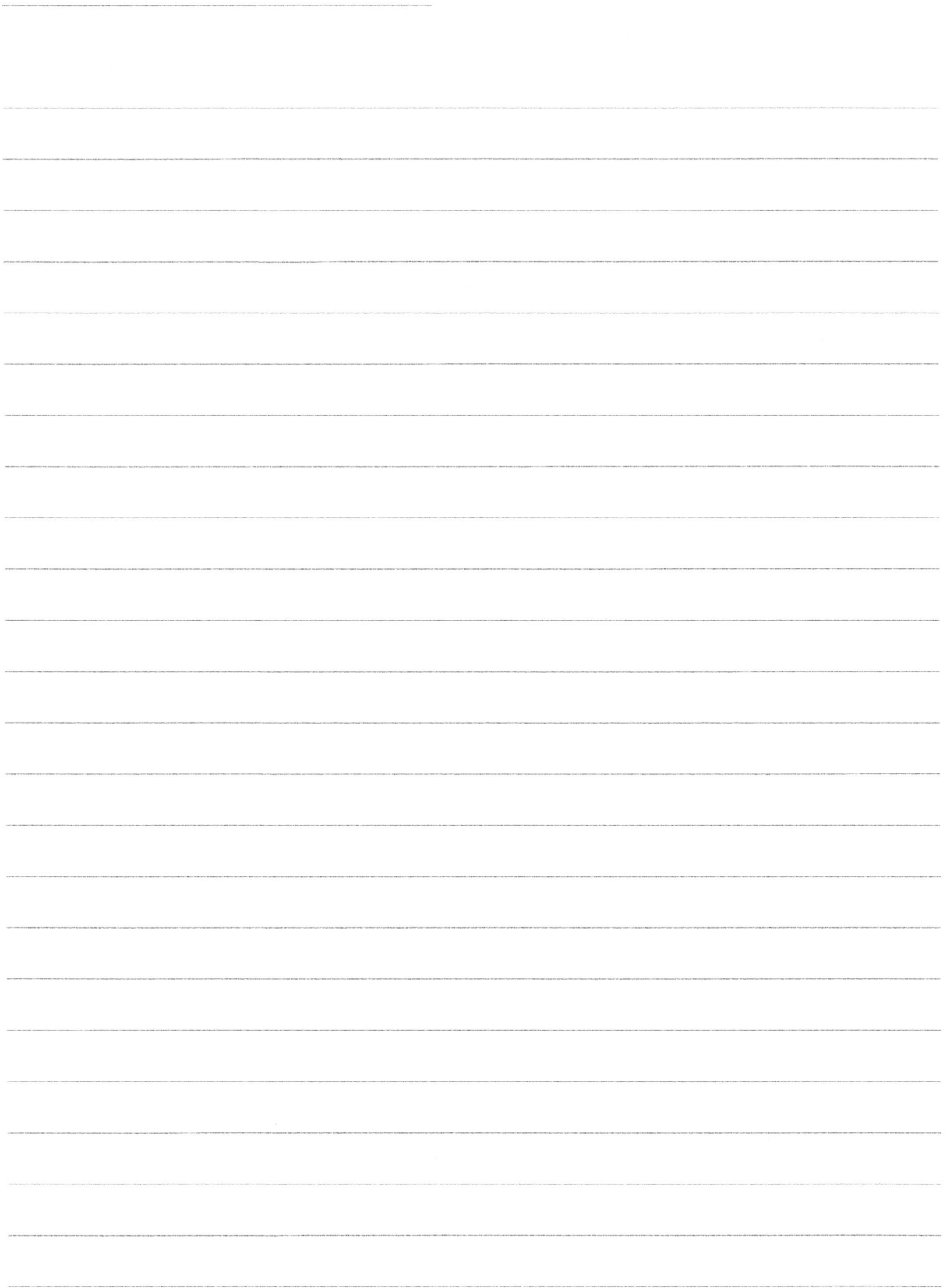

SPIRIT GUIDE MY FEET

DATE

But the Advocate, the Holy Spirit...will teach you all things and will remind you of everything...John 14:26

HOLY SPIRIT THANK YOU FOR:

HOLY SPIRIT TEACH ME...

HOLY SPIRIT REMIND ME...

Proverbs 31 Verse 18: She perceives that her merchandise is good, and her lamp does not go out by night.

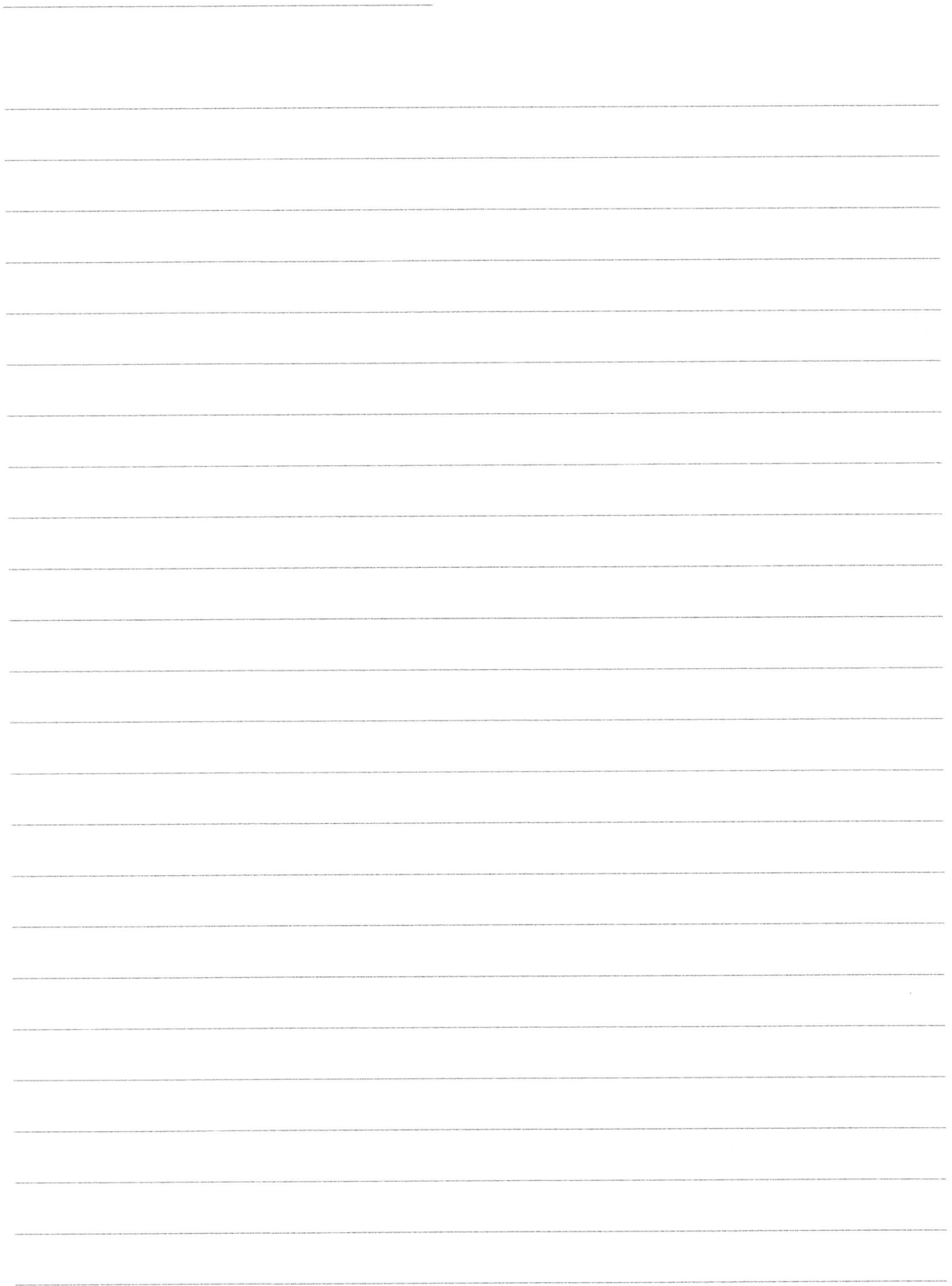

Random Thoughts, ideas, and inspirations...

In this moment, I am Grateful for

_____
_____
_____
_____
_____

Personal Challenges

_____
_____
_____
_____
_____

Prayers for Our Government

_____
_____
_____
_____
_____

Reflections

Date

_____

People To Pray For

_____
_____
_____
_____
_____
_____
_____
_____
_____
_____
_____
_____

_____
_____
_____
_____
_____

SPIRIT GUIDE MY FEET

DATE

But the Advocate, the Holy Spirit...will teach you all
things and will remind you of everything...John 14:26

HOLY SPIRIT THANK YOU FOR:

HOLY SPIRIT TEACH ME...

HOLY SPIRIT REMIND ME...

Blessed is she who has believed that the Lord would fulfill his promises to her! (Luke 1:45)

SPIRIT GUIDE MY FEET

DATE

But the Advocate, the Holy Spirit...will teach you all things and will remind you of everything...John 14:26

HOLY SPIRIT THANK YOU FOR:

HOLY SPIRIT TEACH ME...

HOLY SPIRIT REMIND ME...

God is within her, she will not fall. God will help her at break of day. (Ps. 46:5)

SPIRIT GUIDE MY FEET

DATE

But the Advocate, the Holy Spirit...will teach you all things and will remind you of everything...John 14:26

HOLY SPIRIT THANK YOU FOR:

HOLY SPIRIT TEACH ME...

HOLY SPIRIT REMIND ME...

And the God of all grace, who called you to his eternal glory in Christ,
after you have suffered a little while, will himself restore you and make
you strong, firm and steadfast.. (1 Pet. 5:10)

_____

_____

_____

_____

_____

_____

_____

_____

_____

_____

_____

_____

_____

_____

_____

_____

_____

_____

_____

_____

_____

Random Thoughts, ideas, and inspirations...

In this moment, I am Grateful for

Date
_____

_____
_____
_____
_____
_____

People To Pray For

_____

Personal Challenges

_____
_____
_____
_____
_____
_____
_____
_____

Prayers for Our Government

_____
_____
_____
_____
_____

Reflections

_____
_____
_____
_____
_____
_____

SPIRIT GUIDE MY FEET

DATE

But the Advocate, the Holy Spirit...will teach you all things and will remind you of everything...John 14:26

HOLY SPIRIT THANK YOU FOR:

HOLY SPIRIT TEACH ME...

HOLY SPIRIT REMIND ME...

My beloved is radiant and ruddy, outstanding among ten thousand.
(Song of Solomon 5:10)

SPIRIT GUIDE MY FEET

DATE

But the Advocate, the Holy Spirit...will teach you all
things and will remind you of everything...John 14:26

Holy Spirit Thank You For:

Holy Spirit teach me...

Holy Spirit remind me...

I will praise thee-for I am fearfully and wonderfully made: marvellous are thy works- and that my soul knoweth right well. (Psalm 139:14)

SPIRIT GUIDE MY FEET

DATE

But the Advocate, the Holy Spirit...will teach you all
things and will remind you of everything...John 14:26

HOLY SPIRIT THANK YOU FOR:

HOLY SPIRIT TEACH ME...

HOLY SPIRIT REMIND ME...

Keep me as the apple of the eye, hide me under the shadow of thy wings. (Psalm 17:8)

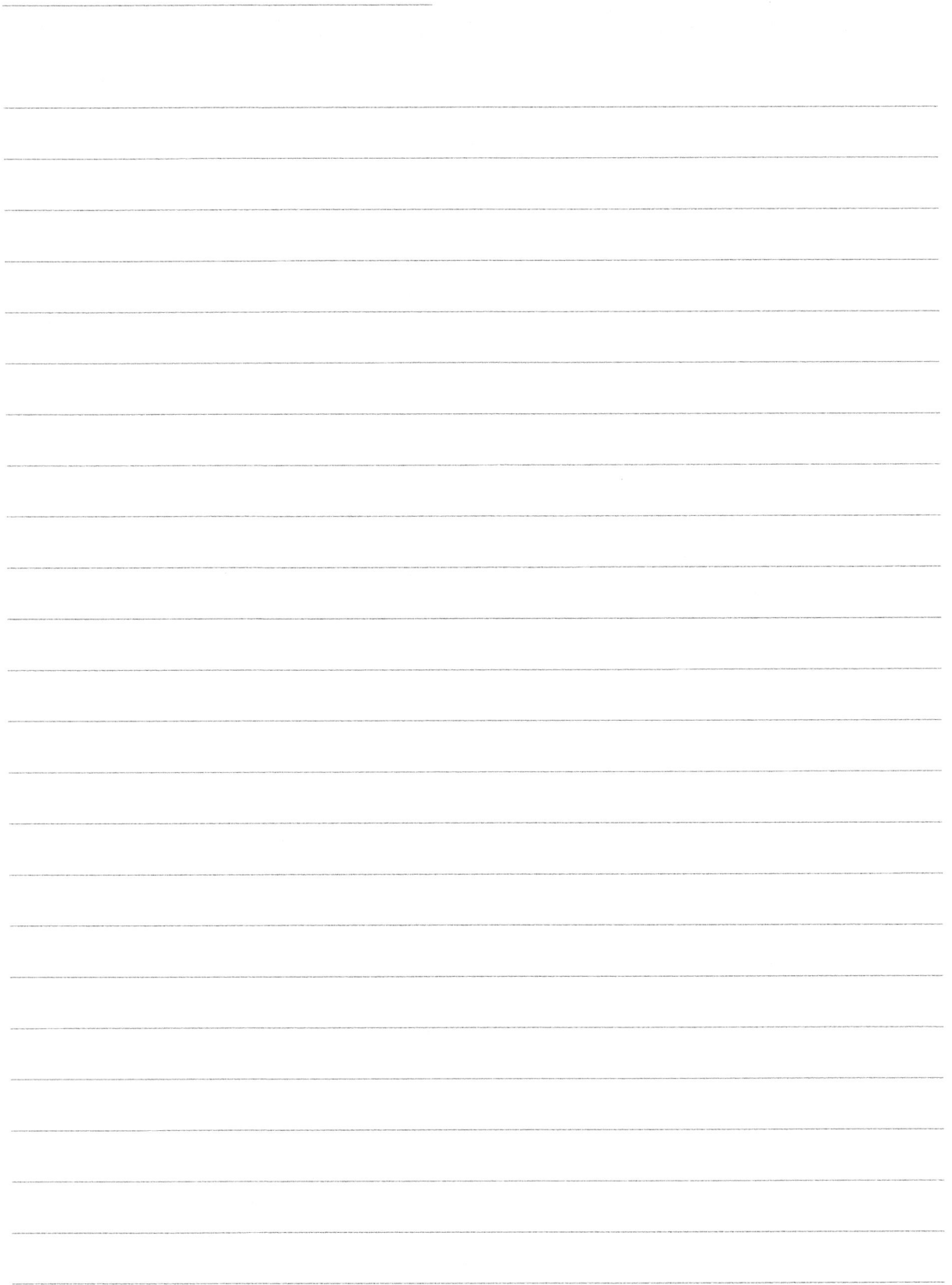

In this moment, I am Grateful for

Date

_____

People To Pray For

Personal Challenges

Prayers for Our Government

Reflections

Random Thoughts, ideas,
and inspirations...

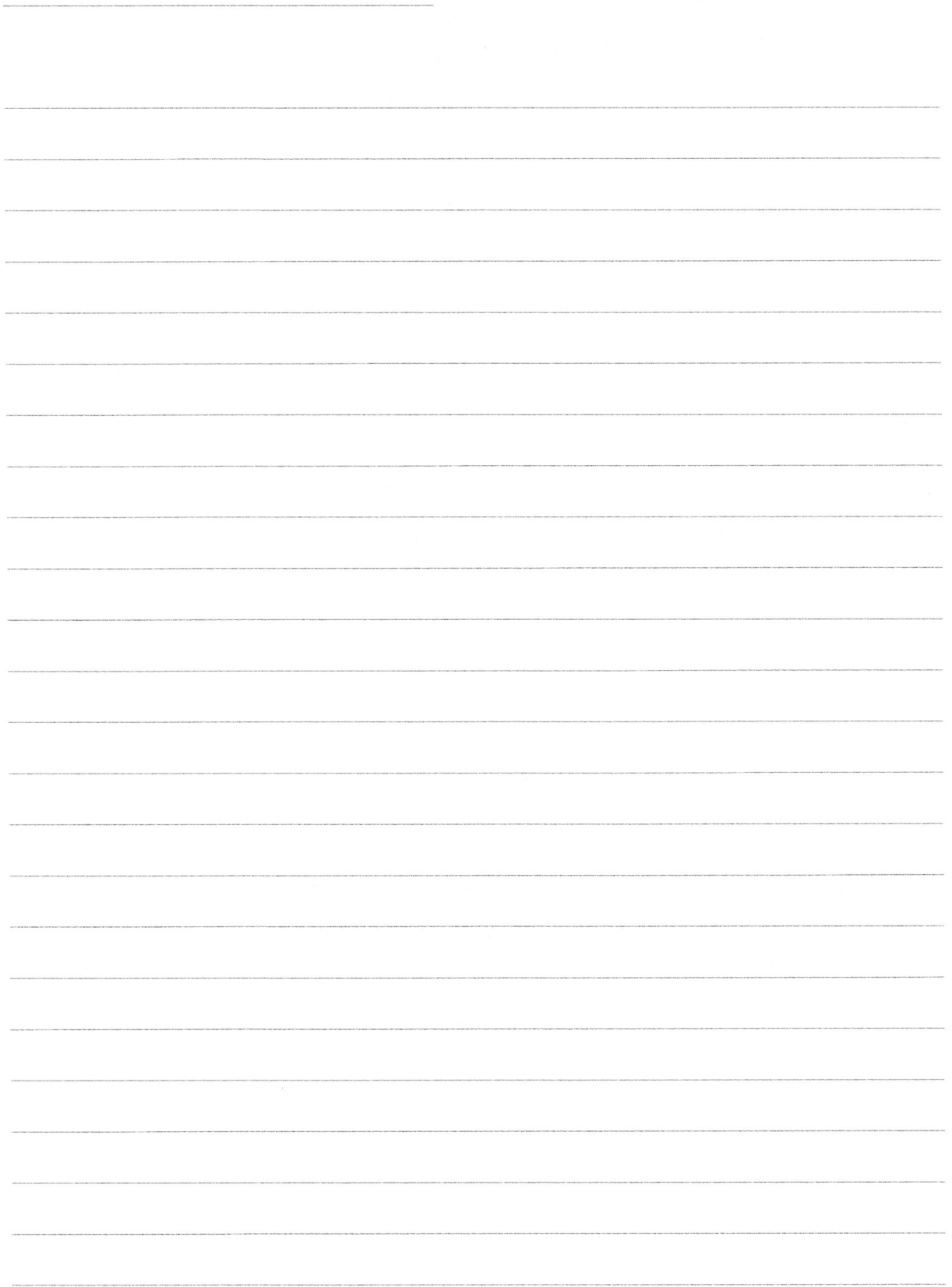

Random Thoughts, ideas, and inspirations...

Thank You For

_____
_____
_____
_____
_____

Personal Challenges

_____
_____
_____
_____
_____

Society And Government

_____
_____
_____
_____

Reflections

_____
_____
_____
_____
_____

Date

_____

People To Pray For

_____
_____
_____
_____
_____
_____
_____
_____
_____
_____
_____
_____
_____

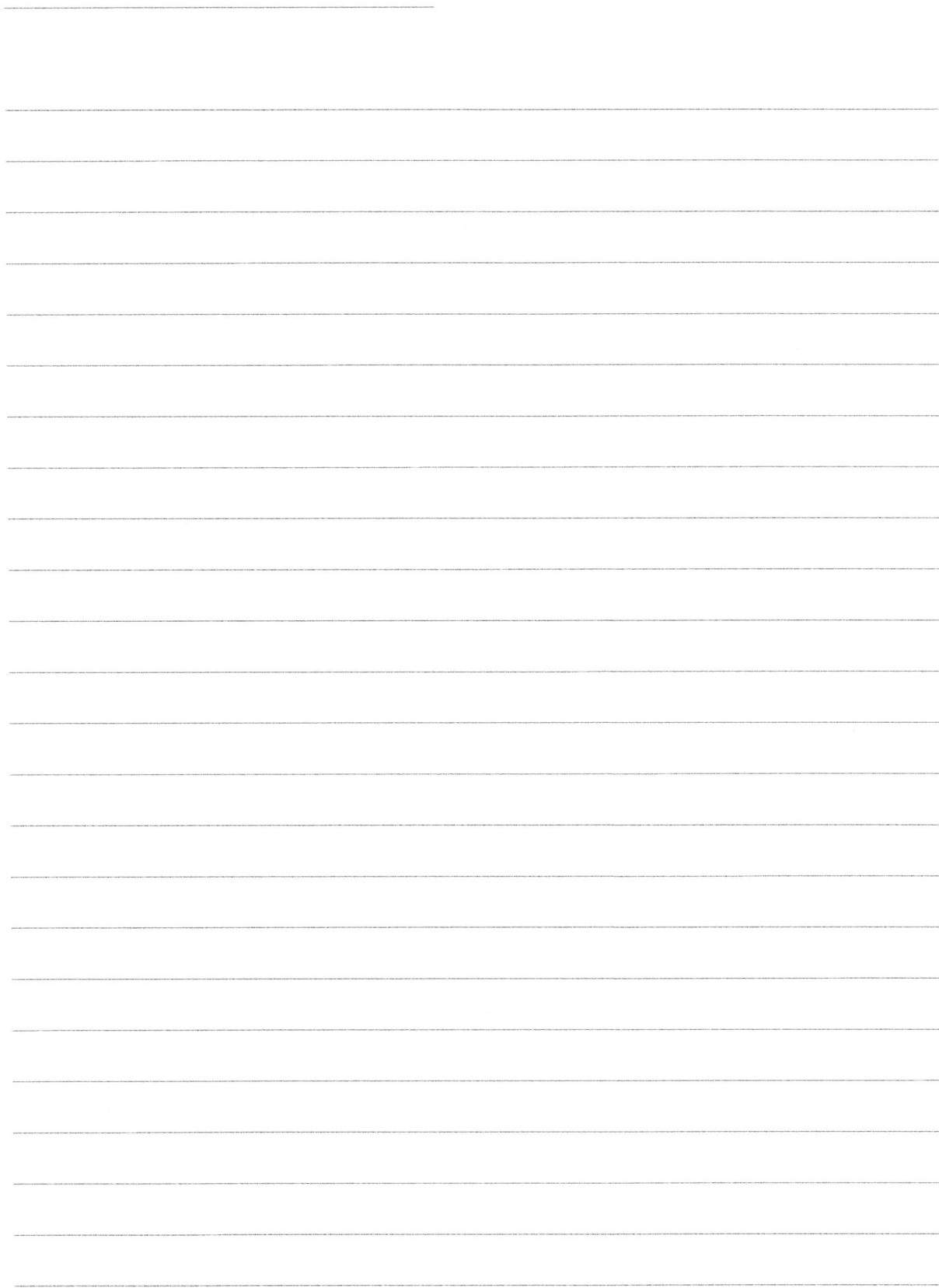

Random Thoughts, ideas, and inspirations...

In this moment, I am Grateful for

Date

_____

_____

_____

_____

_____

People To Pray For

_____

_____

Personal Challenges

_____

_____

_____

_____

_____

_____

_____

_____

_____

_____

_____

Prayers for Our Government

_____

_____

_____

_____

_____

_____

_____

_____

Reflections

_____

_____

_____

_____

_____

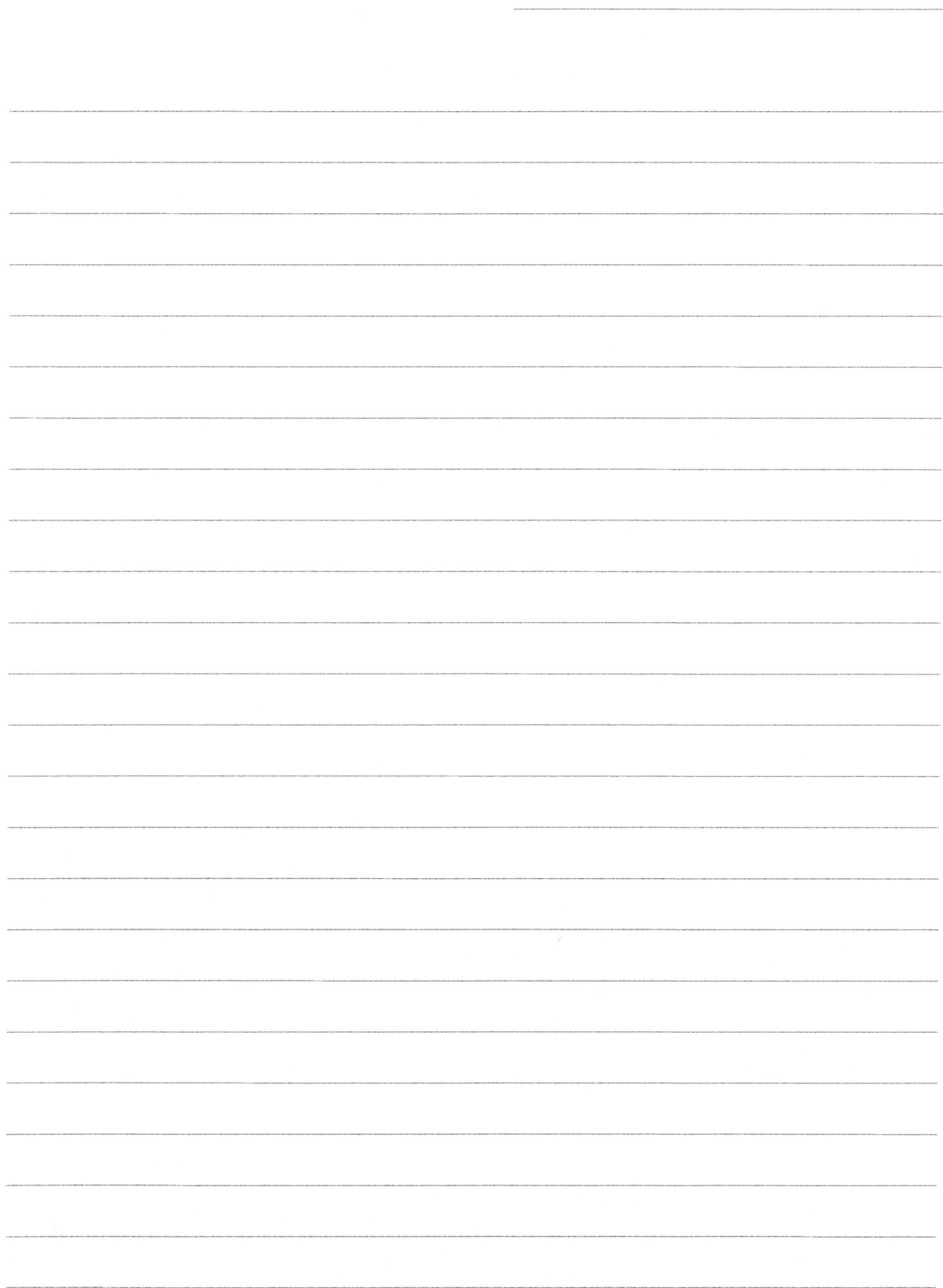

Random Thoughts, ideas, and inspirations...

In this moment, I am Grateful for

Date

People To Pray For

Personal Challenges

Prayers for Our Government

Reflections

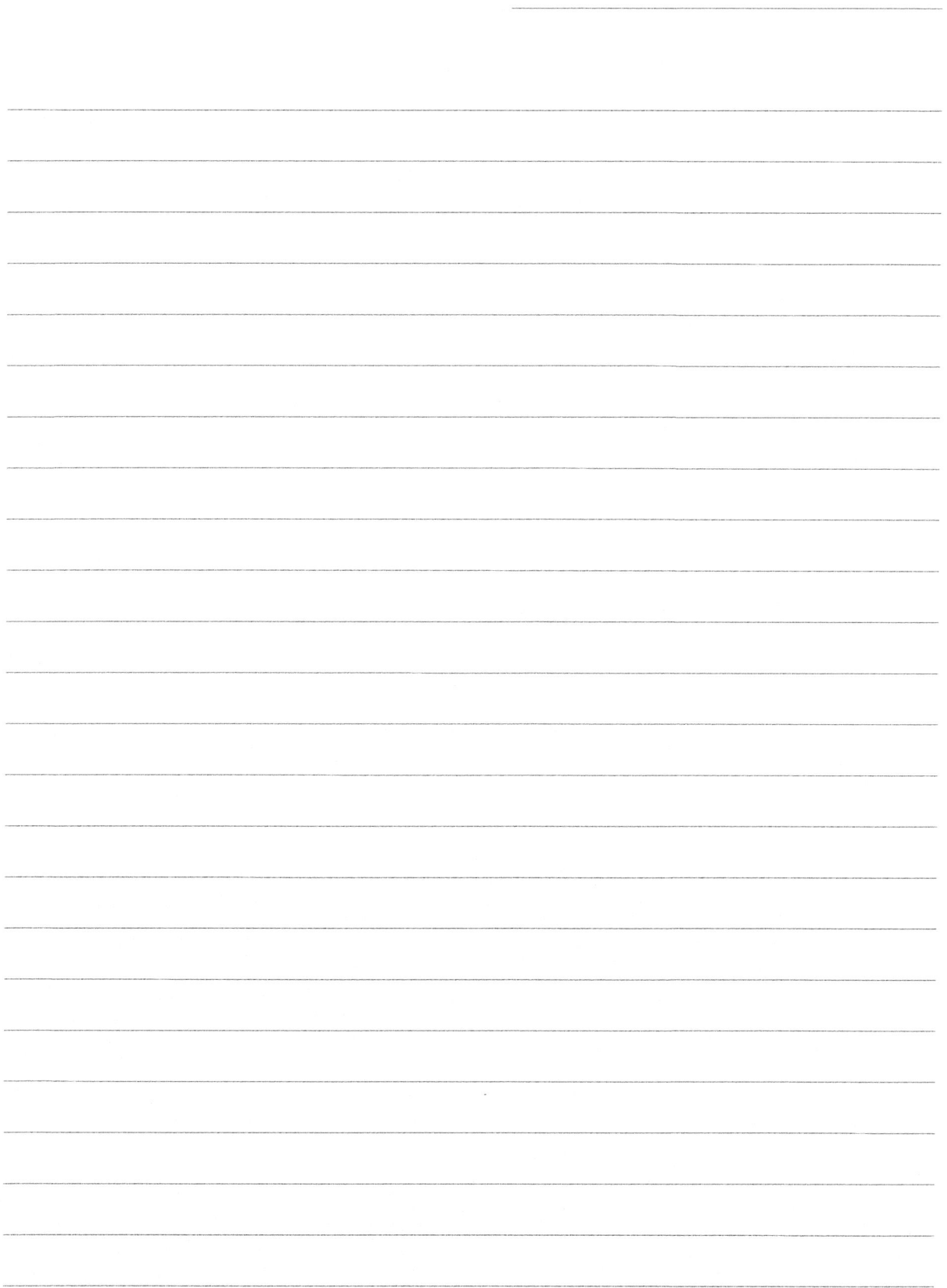

Thank You For

_____
_____
_____
_____
_____

Personal Challenges

_____
_____
_____
_____
_____

Society And Government

_____
_____
_____
_____

Reflections

_____
_____
_____
_____

Date

_____

People To Pray For

_____
_____
_____
_____
_____
_____
_____
_____
_____
_____
_____

Random Thoughts, ideas, and inspirations...

In this moment, I am Grateful for

_____
_____
_____
_____
_____

Personal Challenges

_____
_____
_____
_____
_____

Prayers for Our Government

_____
_____
_____
_____
_____

Reflections

Date

_____

People To Pray For

_____
_____
_____
_____
_____
_____
_____
_____
_____
_____
_____
_____
_____

_____
_____
_____
_____
_____

Random Thoughts, ideas, and inspirations...

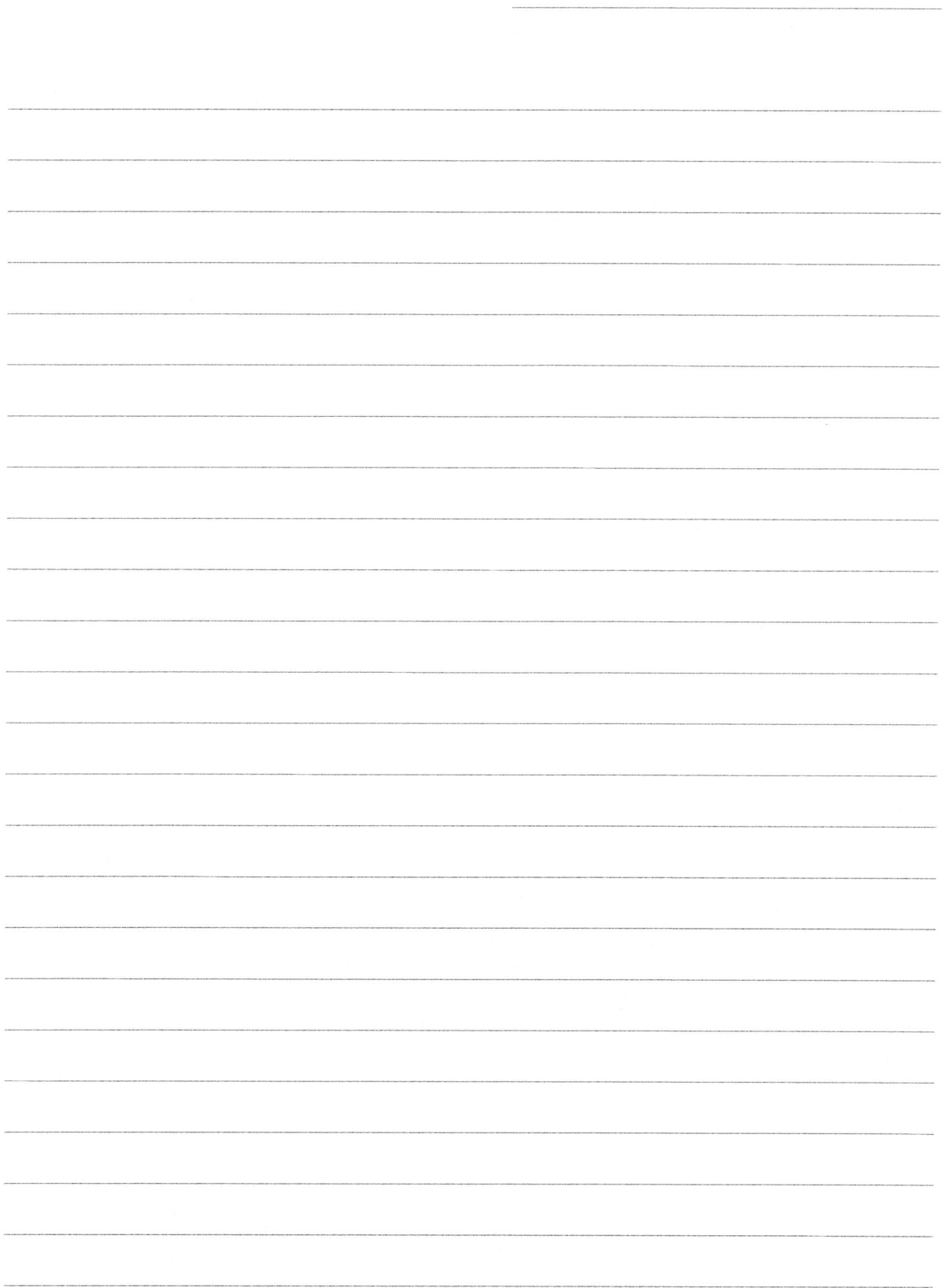

Random Thoughts, ideas, and inspirations...

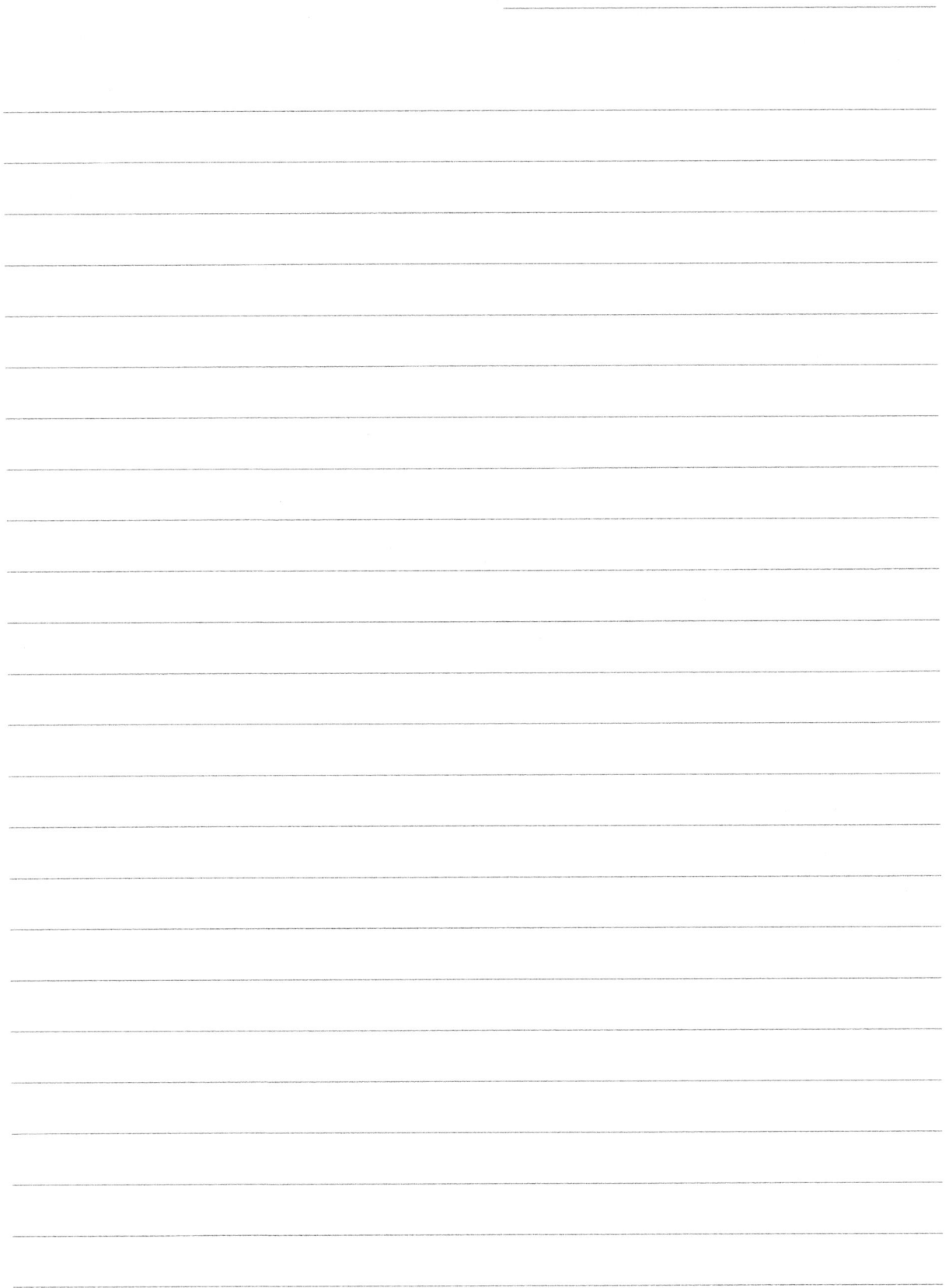

SPIRIT GUIDE MY FEET

DATE

But the Advocate, the Holy Spirit...will teach you all
things and will remind you of everything...John 14:26

HOLY SPIRIT THANK YOU FOR:

HOLY SPIRIT TEACH ME...

HOLY SPIRIT REMIND ME...

Other Journals To Consider

I Love Me Unconditionally
Self Empowering Motivational
Guided Journal For Women

No Weapon Formed Against
This Queen Will Ever Prosper
Blank Journal

I Am Amazing, Angelic, Aligned,
Ambitious & Awakened: The I Am
Journal

More Journals To Come!

Made in the USA
Las Vegas, NV
12 January 2022

41191279R00109